BIBLE HEROINES

DEBORAH/RUTH/ESTHER
MARY, MOTHER OF JESUS

BARBOUR
PUBLISHING, INC.
Uhrichsville, Ohio

Published by Barbour Publishing, Inc., P.O. Box 719, Uhrichsville, Ohio 44683
http://www.barbourbooks.com

 Member of the
Evangelical Christian
Publishers Association

Printed in the United States of America.

CONTENTS

DEBORAH

JUDGE OF ISRAEL

by Carol Fitzpatrick

CHAPTER 1

Shaded by a time-weathered palm tree, Deborah longed for a cool afternoon breeze. God had chosen her as the political and spiritual leader of her people, the Israelites. Day after day, she settled their disputes in this sweltering desert setting.

Sometimes, when she wasn't answering questions, she'd think about all the hardships her people had undergone, for they'd had difficulty learning how to obey God's commands. In fact, their relationship with God had been more like a runaway cart with no sense of direction racing down a steep hill into a great valley.

Because Deborah relied on God's help for every decision, she gave the people wise solutions to their problems. She knew that as long as they turned to God, the Israelites would have strength against their enemies and could easily defeat them in battle.

When Deborah's long day of judging issues had come to a close, she left her place under the palm tree and walked to her home in the village of Ephraim. All of the areas surrounding this land belonged to the twelve tribes of Jacob, who had been renamed Israel by God. Each of Israel's twelve sons had been given a portion of land. Along the way, Deborah scooped up a handful of dirt, slowly sifting it through her fingers back to the ground. *Please give us back the freedom of our land, Lord God,* she prayed silently, knowing that only God could turn their hearts toward Him.

Once back home, Deborah planned the supper she would prepare for her husband, Lapidoth. How she appreciated the fact that he was a quiet man who encouraged her in the work that God had called her to do. Tonight she'd roast a tender piece of lamb and serve it with savory beans and lentils, along with barley bread.

As usual, Lapidoth would probably rush out into the street and beckon several neighborhood men to come and eat with him, for he and Deborah had no children, and in their culture the men and women did not eat meals together.

As the men enjoyed dinner, they routinely discussed the great political issues facing their countrymen. Deborah learned much about what was on their minds as she listened quietly from the kitchen area, ready to bring more food. Sometimes her roles as judge and wife must have been difficult for her to separate.

"When Ehud judged our people, they accepted God's rule over them, but since Ehud died, the Israelites have once again begun the destructive cycle of disobedience, idolatry, and immorality. These actions have made slaves of us," pronounced one of the men, loudly.

"It is King Jabin, the Canaanite, who has oppressed our people," answered another of Lapidoth's dinner guests, unwilling to shoulder any blame upon Israel.

"It is him we must fight against," added the chubby little man with a long beard.

Deborah knew the first man had spoken more correctly.

Since the death of Ehud, a previous judge, the people had become wicked. They had disobeyed God's commandments, rejecting Him as their rightful King. They had even built altars to false gods, such as Baal and Ashtaroth, like the pagan nations around them. And they had chosen marriage partners from the enemies surrounding them.

Since they had picked people who didn't believe in the true God, the Lord had become greatly angered because He knew it would turn the hearts of His people far from Him.

Finally, they had forgotten about God altogether, refusing either to worship Him or to heed His warnings. This failure had removed them from God's protection. As a result, for twenty years the Israelites had been crying out for a deliverer.

Now Deborah had been chosen to lead the people. Their deep concerns were also her own. She knew that the people were doing evil in the sight of the Lord. It broke her heart as she realized their sin.

Arriving at the palm tree before daybreak, Deborah knelt down and began praying even more diligently for her people. "Lord God, you know that the people are afraid of the enemies that surround us. Normal life in our villages has all but ceased, and we cannot move about freely because the roads are no longer safe to travel. Please shine Your light on the path that I am to follow. Use Your strong and mighty hand to save us from those who seek to harm and enslave us. Please hear the cries of Your people, the sons of Israel, and be our deliverer."

As the brilliant sun began to peek over the hillside, the

people started climbing upward, keeping the lush, green palm branches in sight. They came from the nearby cities of Ramah and Bethel.

Now Deborah stood and brushed splotches of the rich earth from her long white tunic and cloak, making sure the veil covered her dark, wavy hair. All day Deborah heard accounts of the afflictions of those living in this area, because as men turned away from God, they also turned against their fellowmen.

Although Deborah had no children of her own, she was considered to be "a mother in Israel," tenderly caring for this flock of people. As a mother would do, she worked tirelessly on their behalf, praying that God would soon wipe away their tears and misery.

Deborah knew that war with their enemies was inevitable. *How will my people defend themselves?* she wondered. None of the forty thousand men in Israel had any weapons. Yet the Canaanites, who surrounded and oppressed them, had many men and numerous weapons. Now Deborah began praying that the Lord would send not only brave men, but also the provisions that the Israelites would need for this war so that His people could be victorious. She also prayed for the commanders whom God would choose to lead this battle.

Through all the prayers that Deborah had been praying, God was filling her spirit with hope. Although she still did not know the substance of His plan for Israel, she began to have the assurance that He indeed heard the cries of His people. A song began to rise up inside of her. She often sang when she prayed, just as King David would do, much later in Israel's history. The more she thought about what the Lord had done in the past, the more confident Deborah became that God would miraculously intervene.

At night, while she walked home, these songs would come forth. Others from their village began to walk and to sing along with Deborah. Deliverance was in the air, and the people breathed the freshness of freedom as they walked through the tall grass on the hillside. As they hiked along the well-worn trails, their leather sandals seemed to have springs.

Of course, there were also the scoffers, those who ridiculed saying, "The Canaanites are too strong. We'll never be able to overthrow them."

Those who sat with Deborah under the palm tree began to feel a new sense of purpose. The number of people grew every day, until the hilltop was covered with those who were dedicated to God and came to pray for Israel.

Deborah reminded them of the fact that God's mighty power had delivered the children of Israel out of bondage to Egypt, after they'd been there four hundred years. God had already proven, in Israel's past, that He was stronger than all the false gods to which the people had been praying. Now they wondered how they could ever have been so foolish as to listen to the Canaanites, instead of their own powerful God. But this repeated sin of the Israelites kept an endless cycle of pain going on for many years. Yet no matter how many times they returned to God, they still kept turning back to false gods, which had never worked in the first place.

"How long will they continue to be so stubborn and hard-headed?" Deborah wondered, looking up to the sky, as though she were asking God directly.

In Israel, everyone's name had a meaning. Little Jewish girls were given names of beautiful objects in nature or pleasant graces of character. Deborah's name meant "bee," and God was about to use this strong characteristic in her to deliver a real sting to the forces of evil that now surrounded them.

CHAPTER 2

Although life for the Israelites was extremely difficult, Deborah had come to realize that God was testing them. This was the reason He had not driven out the nations that persecuted them. Would Israel finally give up their idolatry and worship God as their only King? Were they willing to obey so that God could deliver them?

Early one morning, as Deborah sat praying beneath her palm tree, she began to hear God's clear command for Israel. This was the message and plan for which she had waited, for her call, as Israel's judge, was to lead the people into battle against those who were attempting to destroy them. She never wanted to take action unless she knew for sure it was the Lord's will.

God's rescue of Israel would also involve a man named Barak, whose name meant "lightning." He was a military commander in Israel, a general. The son of Abinoam, Barak was from Kedesh-naphtali, a city to the north of Ephraim. Deborah now had to confront Barak with God's special news. She prayed for both the words she'd need to say and the outcome of this meeting, for she needed God to prepare Barak with courage.

Although Israel in times past had had a very powerful army, they hadn't fought a big battle in a long time. Now the men didn't even have weapons. "How can we possibly overthrow King Jabin's forces?" Deborah asked God in her heart.

The Lord reminded her of how He had used the Egyptian Pharaoh's army to be swallowed up by the Red Sea, so that Moses and the children of Israel could cross over it safely. So although Deborah didn't as yet understand the whole plan, she did already know two things: first, that God's power had no limitations, and second, that He was always truthful.

Deborah's job was to trust, and God's job was to make this victory over their enemy become a reality, no matter how lop-sided the odds appeared to her human eyes. Deborah knew that if she spent time dwelling on the facts before her, she, too, might become paralyzed with fear, because the only military forces Israel had were two tribal hill groups of soldiers.

Deborah's strong spiritual character traits, however, were the obvious foundation of her success as a military leader, wife, judge, and prophetess; and one of her strongest attri-butes, her obedience to God, would open the door for Israel's deliverance.

Deborah did not disclose all of God's plan to the people because they might have tried to force the issue before God had made Barak ready. Instead, Deborah guided the Israelites to begin praying for those who would lead them in the upcoming battle. Knowing that many men might lose their lives once the war began, Deborah encouraged every-one to ask for God's mercy upon their casualties.

Day after day the people gathered around Deborah, under the palm tree, and most of them were so busy praying that they no longer had time for disputes. God was truly preparing His people. The prayers had changed their attitudes, and the people had even begun asking God to forgive their wicked ways. Arriving at their homes at night, they had become more loving to their families.

People from surrounding villages, including some of their enemies, began to notice a distinct difference in the character of the Israelites. Only months before they had acted like "true slaves," cowering away from those who oppressed them.

Now confidence and expectation seemed to permeate the very air they breathed. They walked with pride and purpose, heads held high, as they approached Deborah each day. Together they prayed beneath her palm tree.

Those who came to Deborah's house to share the evening meal with Lapidoth now talked of possibilities. "The people appear to be getting strong," said the chubby man with the long white beard.

"Yes," agreed a thinner man with a dark brown robe and a merry twinkle in his eyes. "But we wonder just who will lead us into battle," he said with one thick brown eyebrow curling upward like a question mark.

"Who would dare to come against Sisera, the commander of King Jabin's forces?" asked a third man who was seated next to Lapidoth. He seemed to tremble even at the thought of what he'd just uttered.

Hearing the men from the doorway of the kitchen, Deborah wanted to shout out Barak's name. But she kept silent, waiting for God to finalize the plans.

"God will take care of these details," stated Lapidoth confidently, although he had no name to give them.

A cold chill ran down Deborah's spine as she considered Sisera. He commanded the troops of Jabin, the king of the Canaanites, who reigned in a place called Hazor.

Sisera had over nine hundred chariots. How could the Israelites fight against such power? Besides that, King Jabin had thousands of soldiers.

Just thinking about how outnumbered the Israelites were scared Deborah, but she gave her fears to God, knowing that He was not taking her into this battle to lose. Their victory was assured. "Lord, help me, even when I find it difficult to trust," Deborah prayed.

Sometimes the secret God had entrusted to her made her feel very lonely and isolated, because she could not share the things she knew in her heart until the right moment. Day after day, she continued to wait on God.

She knew that He continued to love the Israelites although they had turned away from Him. God had blessed them with children even when they followed in the ways of the nations around them, teaching their children to worship idols. Tears streamed down Deborah's cheeks as she pictured all the precious children who had been dedicated to the Ashtoreth statue and brought up to serve these false gods.

How could God still love the Israelites? Especially after they had taken His greatest gifts—their children—and taught them to worship idols. What a terrible sin it was. But then every person in Israel was guilty of some kind of sin, and all of them needed deliverance from God. Now Deborah began to pray that God would turn the hearts of her people back to Him. They always cried out loudly enough for His help when they were miserable! Yet now she wondered if they were truly willing to give up their wicked ways and obediently follow Him. "Forgive us and enable us to seek Your ways, O God," Deborah prayed.

Sometimes it was hard for Deborah to understand why God had chosen her, especially when she felt weak and scared. Then she'd remember that the outcome of the battle didn't depend on her. She simply had to be willing to take the risk. God's power would bring the desired results, just as He'd said.

"What has God told you of His plan?" asked the people who surrounded Deborah under the palm tree.

"Soon you will know," she answered, and then began reminding them again of the ways God had rescued their people in the past. "Don't you remember when Othniel, another of Israel's judges, went out to war?" she asked. "The Lord gave the king of Mesopotamia into his hands," she added, rapping one hand with her fist as if to demonstrate God's fury at this enemy of Israel. "Then there was peace in Israel for forty years. God will bring about such peace again. He is waiting to see His people turn to Him with faithful hearts."

Deborah looked out over the large number of Israelites before her. Now they dotted the whole top of the hillside. She remembered the small group who had first come to pray for Israel. How their numbers had grown, and yet there were so many more in Israel who had to be willing to allow God to remake their hearts of stone. As the sun began to slip down lower on the horizon, a cool, refreshing breeze blew across their midst, as if to remind Deborah that God watched over all of them. She lifted her eyes to heaven and led the people in a prayer of gratitude.

CHAPTER 3

Deborah couldn't sleep that night, for she sensed that God was about to set His plan in motion. After tossing and turning for hours, she arose early and climbed the hill to pray beneath her beloved palm tree. As the sun's warmth washed over her, God finally told her it was time to enlist the help of Barak. Although Deborah hadn't wasted a moment while waiting on the Lord to initiate His plan, she felt both relief and terror at this word from Him. She'd finally received permission to move forward, but this plan would involve the lives of everyone in her country!

Writing a note and sealing it with hot wax, Deborah dispatched the message that would summon Barak. While she waited for it to be delivered, she prayed. First, she prayed that Barak would have a willing heart, and second, she asked that God would give him an abundance of courage. This general would need both for the task at hand.

Barak, the son of a man named Abinoam, lived in a place called Kedesh-naphtali, which was to the north of the Sea of Galilee. It took some time for him to travel to where Deborah waited.

The people surrounding Deborah beneath the palm tree began to realize that her mood seemed somehow different. Perhaps she had news to relate to them. Patiently, they watched and prayed with her. Finally, toward evening, they sang a new song with Deborah. It stirred their minds and hearts with anticipation.

The next morning Deborah again woke early, preparing a basket of fruit and bread. Her sandals stepped lightly, as though nearly floating on top of the dirt road that led to the hill. When she reached the summit, Barak and some of his soldiers were waiting for her. They nodded politely as she approached, allowing her to speak first.

Deborah inhaled a deep breath. She hoped she'd remember every word that God had spoken to her so that the message would be given forth correctly.

"Behold, the Lord, the God of Israel, has commanded, 'Go and march to Mount Tabor, and take with you ten thousand men from the sons of Naphtali and from the sons of Zebulun. And I will draw out to you Sisera, the commander of Jabin's army, with his chariots and his many troops to the river Kishon; and I will give him into your hand.' "

Deborah sighed with relief. Finally, she'd delivered God's message to Barak. How would he react?

Barak looked pale and stricken, as though he'd just been slugged in the stomach by a giant. Why should he feel such apprehension? After all, his job was to be a military leader. Perhaps it was the great odds at stake. Perhaps also the fact that King Jabin had the finest chariots and equipment, not to mention that his soldiers were extremely well trained.

Barak gulped before speaking, hoping he didn't sound too cowardly as his voice quivered. "If you go with me, then I will go; but if you will not go with me, I will not go."

Perhaps he doesn't understand that the victory is assured, Deborah pondered. In that moment she also realized that her faith in God's ability ran much deeper than Barak's.

Carefully she considered her response as she placed her life and well-being into God's hand. "I will surely go with you; nevertheless, the honor shall not be yours on the journey that you are about to take, for the Lord will sell Sisera into the hands of a woman."

Barak looked around at the men who were with him, waiting to see their reaction. However, they yelled their approval in one loud cheer. Finally, they would overthrow the Canaanites who had oppressed them for so long. If God Himself had chosen a woman to lead them, then who were they to argue?

Those from the neighboring towns, who now lined the hill and had overheard this exchange, began to cheer as well. The earth beneath them seemed to shake as people began to stomp their feet and dance, unable to contain their excitement. Now they spilled down the hill, carrying the news to others. "Victory is assured; Deborah will lead us!" they shouted.

Lapidoth's heart sank. What if all of Israel was successful, but he lost Deborah in the process? Being a man of few words, he'd never told his wife how much she meant to him or how proud he was of her. Would he ever get the chance?

Deborah stood up and went with Barak to Kedesh, where they awaited the troops who would come together for battle. Meanwhile, Barak sent a message to the men in Zebulun and Naphtali to meet him in Kedesh. Over ten thousand men from these two regions of the sons of Israel amassed for combat.

Deborah led them in prayer before she explained all that God had done and would do for Israel, the people He loved.

Barak leaned against a tree and stroked his beard. In his heart he knew full well how close Deborah stayed to God. That was why he'd selfishly wanted the assurance that she'd go with him to Kadesh, not only to guarantee that the presence of God would indeed be with them in battle, but also because she was so charismatic with the people. What a great lesson in humility he was about to learn!

God had already begun to set in motion the events that would lead to Sisera's downfall. A man named Heber, who was a Kenite, had separated himself from his people. He had pitched his tent far away, near the large oak tree in Zaanaim, which is near Kedesh. Somewhere back in this man's family line was Hobag, the father-in-law of Moses. The Bible does not reveal why Heber wished to be away from his people, but he was a friend of Sisera.

Watching all these preparations, he decided to warn Sisera about the attack that was about to be waged on him by the Israelites. So Heber went to Sisera, relating to him that Barak had gone up to Mount Tabor with many troops.

Hearing this news, Sisera called together all of his chariots. What a sight, as over nine hundred chariots and all their drivers lined up along the river Kishon! What a force to be reckoned with! Who in their right minds would even try to come against them?

This is exactly what Barak began to think. He stayed on

Mount Tabor with his ten thousand men, not moving down toward the confrontation that awaited them at the river Kishon.

Deborah watched all of this and realized the troops were not advancing. Straight she went to Barak, placed her hands on her hips, and boldly said, "Arise! For this is the day in which the Lord has given Sisera into your hands; behold, the Lord has gone out before you."

Barak was trapped. Either he went down to the battle or he lost his reputation as a military leader altogether. Fearfully, Barak led his men down Mount Tabor toward the riverbank. Why couldn't he bring himself just to trust that God would indeed come through for the Israelites? His inward struggle grew greater with each step down the mountain.

Deborah smiled, keenly aware that all those days of prayer had prepared her to watch for God's miracle. She'd never known exactly how He would answer Israel's prayer, because God hadn't told her, but she knew the outcome would be spectacular. She knew that when God intervened in the lives of His people, she could anticipate something truly unique, incredible, and powerful.

As the trumpet blasts sounded, signaling that Israel had gone to war, Deborah prayed, "Lord, these men have volunteered to be in Your army. Now do as You've said and give them this victory. They have no weapons. You alone are their rock and their shield. Fight for us, O mighty God!"

The mountain began to quake and men trembled at the presence of the Lord, Who had come to fight Israel's war against their enemy. Ominous gray clouds formed above the river as the heavens began pouring forth a deluge of water. Then the angels of heaven began to fight the battle, as torrents of rain caused the earth beneath the horses' hooves to fall away in huge chunks.

Although Deborah didn't go down to the front lines of the battle, she seems to have held these timid Hebrew tribesmen together by both the force of her own words and also her conviction in God's ability. From her vantage point, at the base camp they'd established high on the mountain, she continued to pray for the safety of her countrymen. A heavy burden weighed on her heart, for it had been reliance on the words of the Lord spoken through her that had united the tribes of Israel in this place.

Deborah relished God's nearness and power. *How unending is His love for Israel,* she thought, then she wrapped her arms snugly around herself, not only as a shield against the unrelenting wintry wind but also because God's closeness made a sudden tingle go down her spine.

Shortly after the battle began, a deluge of rain and hail obscured Deborah's view of the battlefront. She could only imagine what took place moment by moment. The mountain quaked from the thundering presence of the Lord in their midst, for He had dispatched angels to fight for Israel. This would have terrified Deborah were it not for the fact that she held as a treasured gift God's assurance of victory.

While she waited for the outcome of the battle, Deborah considered how God had chosen Israel as His special people and continued to protect them, even when they least deserved

His care. This land that Israel now sought to regain had been given to them by God long ago, for God had communicated this directly with Abraham, saying, "Now lift up your eyes and look from the place where you are, northward and southward and eastward and westward; for all the land which you see, I will give it to you and to your descendants forever."

Above all, Deborah knew God to be faithful to His covenants. Since He had promised the land to the people of Israel, He would assist them in regaining it, because this promise, called a covenant, could not be broken. Although for a time Israel had been unfaithful to God through their disobedience and it had brought them into slavery, God continued to love them.

Thus, no matter how unlikely this victory appeared to be, especially since Israel was so greatly outnumbered, it would be accomplished. Deborah thought about the fact that Abraham had been ninety-nine years old when God had promised him a son. God had even told Abraham what to name his son—Isaac. She chuckled thinking how Abraham's wife, Sarah, had laughed when she'd first heard about God's promise, because she, too, had been very old. One year later, however, that special baby had been born, and the promise of the land had been passed down to Isaac and his descendants.

Deborah remembered the story of Isaac building an altar to the Lord at a place called Beersheba. There the God of Abraham had appeared to Isaac, promising to bless him and his descendants. Then Isaac had become the father of Jacob. Later, God had changed Jacob's name to Israel and blessed him with twelve sons. Each of these twelve sons had become the head of one of the tribes that now made up the nation of Israel. The names of these sons were: Reuben, Simeon, Levi, Judah, Issachar, Zebulun, Dan, Naphtali, Gad, Asher, Joseph, and Benjamin. Each of them had known about God's promise concerning the land of Canaan.

Every time God's people failed to obey, they found themselves in captivity, yet they repeated this process over and over again, failing to recognize their sins before the Lord.

God had called Moses to lead the children of Israel out of bondage in Egypt after four hundred years. Then when they'd nearly reached the land that God had promised them, Moses himself had become disobedient before the Lord. God had not been able to allow this kind of behavior, especially from one He'd chosen to lead the people. Since Moses had failed to follow God's instructions, he had never been permitted to enter the land of Canaan. Instead, Joshua had led the sons of Israel into their land.

God had told the Israelites not only to conquer the people who occupied the land but also to "completely drive them out." This, however, the Israelites did not do. Those who practiced idol worship remained in the land. Then many of the people of Israel married the Canaanites and adopted their evil ways. They turned away from the living God Who had chosen them, nurtured and protected them, and desired to have a relationship with them. Instead, they built idols of wood and stone. This disobedience led to their captivity by others.

As long as they adhered to God's laws, He protected them.

Deborah knew that her people had made a mockery of God's love for them. To the nations around them, the Israelites would boast about their powerful God, but then they proceeded to ignore God and do what was right in their own eyes.

The very enemy that Israel had failed to drive out was the one that they confronted this day in battle. Deborah wanted desperately to see what was going on below the mountain, but the wind and rain continued, creating a thick, gray, cloud-like mist. Beneath a flat rock overhang, she warmed herself by a fire. If only she could hear what was going on below, but the constant crashing of thunder made that impossible.

When the trumpet blast in Israel had first sounded, calling the men to battle, the divisions of the tribe of Reuben had shown great resolve of heart. They'd understood God's strong hand was with them in the fight, and they would not cease from the encounter with Israel's oppressor until the victory had been accomplished.

Deborah considered all those who had come to defend Israel that day. The very princes of Issachar, a tribe near the Sea of Galilee, were with Deborah. They had rushed into the Jezreel valley below, following on Barak's heels.

Deborah felt such a sense of pride in her people today, knowing they were willing to risk their lives to be free. Now the rain beat down even harder, so that neither the chariot riders nor their horses could see. As quickly as the men attempted to wipe the moisture from their eyes, they would be drenched again.

Just when Sisera, who led King Jabin's forces, thought

things couldn't get any worse, round, frozen balls of hail began pelting them. Raising their arms over their heads, the soldiers attempted to shield themselves, but in doing so, they also released the tension on the horses' reins.

Dodging the painful pounding of the hail and no longer able to sense any direction, the horses now began stamping their hooves in place. Rather than moving forward, toward the Israelites, the valiant steeds turned in confusing circles. Riders who attempted to dismount were trampled by their own disoriented geldings.

God had strategically placed the icy, cold wind, rain, and hail to the backs of His people, and they had no problem locating the enemy. They easily repelled the infantry troops and wrested their weapons from them. While Barak's troops continued to advance toward the chariots, they also pushed them ever closer to the edge of the river's raging swell.

CHAPTER 5

Now most of Sisera's nine hundred iron chariots had either been driven into the thick mud, making them immovable, or they had fallen into the swiftly moving current of the river. Most of his riders had leaped off their mounts, leaving the horses to fend for themselves.

God's mighty angels continued to fight the battle for Israel. Sisera, who had trusted in his combat armaments instead of the Lord, finally began to understand that he'd lost the battle. So he slipped away from his chariot, escaping from the battle on foot, and leaving his soldiers alone and without leadership as they lay bleeding and dying across the muddy battlefield.

Meanwhile, the water continued to rise until the Kishon River flooded over its banks, carrying many of Sisera's troops away and drowning them in its swift, whirling current.

Now the scene of the battle began shifting away from the riverbank, as Sisera's army, perplexed without his guidance, began to retreat. Barak's troops pursued the remaining chariots and foot soldiers as far as a place called Harosheth-hagoyim, where the rest of the enemy's men now fell by the edge of the sword. The Israelites had not provoked this war; God had told them to fight. Deborah was convinced that if they had failed to listen, their enemies would have wiped them off the face of the earth.

God had plans for Israel's twelve tribes, therefore, He had

to preserve them. They were the people He had chosen to record and maintain copies of His Word, that it might be given to all future generations. Also, the promised Messiah would someday be born from this line of descendants following Abraham, Isaac, and Jacob, fulfilling God's covenant promise.

The haze of rain and fog finally began to clear as Deborah stood on the mountaintop and peered down into the valley below. As she carefully surveyed the land, the result of God's promised victory became evident. The bodies of those who had refused to heed God's warning and had oppressed and enslaved Israel, now lay stretched out across the river's banks. Deborah wept for the enemy's stubborn disobedience, which had cost them their lives.

God, however, comforted her spirit, reminding her that He had provided ample time for these men to turn from their wicked ways, just as He had done throughout all of history. They had refused either to repent of their evil or to worship Him.

Then God encouraged Deborah, prompting her with the words He'd given her to speak to Barak when He'd first related His plan. "Behold, the Lord, the God of Israel, has commanded, 'Go march to Mount Tabor, and take with you ten thousand men from the sons of Naphtali and from the sons of Zebulun. And I will draw out to you, Sisera, the commander of Jabin's army, with his chariots and his many troops to the river Kishon; and I will give him into your hand.' "

God had indeed given the victory to Israel. The enemy had been utterly wiped out. Surely the nations surrounding them would be speaking of the power of their mighty God.

Deborah's thoughts now turned back to her people. How many had been lost? Was Barak still alive? And what had become of Sisera, the leader of King Jabin's army? Would Barak display the courage to pursue him until the end? Deborah knew as long as Sisera lived, he would remain a threat to Israel.

"Oh Lord, please give Barak the will to finish this battle," Deborah prayed, knowing that she'd been the one who'd had to coax Barak off the mountain in the first place. Barak had surely witnessed God's mighty hand against their enemy. Deborah hoped this display had bolstered Barak's faith.

Now the sun's brilliant rays began peeking through all the gray clouds, a silent witness to the end of the battle. Although the top of the mountain had now begun to warm up, Deborah longed to be sitting under the shade of her palm tree. She desired this familiar place not only for its safety and tranquility, but also for the nearness of those who had so diligently prayed with her about God's plan.

Unable to wonder about the outcome any longer, Deborah began her slow descent from Mount Tabor. Two of Israel's troops had remained nearby, guarding Israel's judge, for the enemy would have liked nothing better than to wipe out Deborah and leave Israel without any leadership. Now the soldiers made sure Deborah safely exited the rocky slopes.

Grasping the edge of a large rock, she began singing a song of thanksgiving to the Lord for sparing her people. When the song was done, she asked, "Please help me find Barak."

Deborah could hardly wait to tell her husband, Lapidoth,

about the outcome of the conflict, for God had only requested ten thousand men to be on the front lines. Now Deborah knew that this, too, had been part of God's unique plan, because if Israel had possessed more weapons and more men, then the nations around them would not have realized the magnitude of this miracle.

On the other hand, Sisera had gone into battle with a massive amount of resources. Still reeling from the affect of his army's devastating defeat, Sisera was too humiliated and terrified to return to King Jabin with this news.

Near a huge oak tree, Sisera sank down onto the muddy ground, placing his head in his hands. Utter despair cast a dark shadow over him, much as the rain clouds had earlier. He knew he could never go home, for how could he possibly explain what had taken place?

The storm, he mused. *I'll tell him about the terrible rain, wind, and hail,* he thought. But then the hard truth hit him full force. *No, I was in charge of the king's forces, and now they're all gone. . .dead.*

What profit could there be to wasting his time looking back at all the battles he'd won for the Canaanites? The only victory that mattered now to King Jabin was this present one. With this defeat, the king's own life would be in jeopardy.

Should Sisera go back and attempt to guard the king? For a few moments he considered this last-ditch effort to be worthy of the confidence that the king had placed in his ability, but then he remembered that the Canaanites didn't negotiate; they conquered!

Sisera was running out of time. The enemy would surely pursue him. Who could have predicted this outcome? Sisera was still stunned by the defeat. *We outnumbered them so heavily, and they didn't have weapons. How could we have lost?* he thought.

After a few moments, Sisera remembered Heber, the Kenite, who had been a friend to King Jabin and had pitched his tent near this ancient oak in Zaanaim. Heber had at least come to warn Sisera that Israel had been amassing their forces for battle. Surely he wanted to stay in the king's favor. *Perhaps he will hide me,* thought Sisera, a man fresh out of options.

CHAPTER 6

Barak and his men had confronted the remainder of Sisera's army in Sisera's hometown of Harosheth-hagoyim. After they had all fallen by the sword, Sisera himself had still not been found.

"The coward has run away!" shouted Barak to his men, seemingly forgetting the fact that Deborah had needed to persuade him to come down from Mount Tabor to fight the battle. More importantly though, her prophecy that "the victory will go to a woman" had also slipped his mind.

Meanwhile, Sisera stood in front of Heber's tent, trying to catch his breath after running so fast. At the same moment, Heber's wife, Jael, opened the flap of the tent and saw Sisera. She greeted him saying, "Turn aside, my master, turn aside to me! Do not be afraid."

She said this to reassure Sisera that he could trust her for help. Gratefully, he followed her into the tent. Cold and wet, he shivered like a lost puppy. Not only had he been deluged by the rainstorm, but he'd also become overheated as he ran. Jael bent down beside the door and retrieved a neatly folded mantle, which was like a robe or a cloak. When Sisera had sat down on the rug that covered the dirt floor, Jael sheltered him with it.

Then he requested of Jael, "Please give me a little water to drink, for I am thirsty."

"Yes, of course," she answered, as she slipped into the kitchen area. She needed time to think this through.

Sisera wouldn't be on her doorstep unless he'd lost the battle, she reasoned. Otherwise, he'd have been off celebrating with his troops. Jael considered all she stood to lose if she helped this enemy of Israel. Her husband, Heber, had separated himself from his own people, but somehow he had managed to maintain a cordial relationship with King Jabin. Heber would never come against Israel, especially once he knew that they'd been victorious over the king's troops.

Heber had left at dawn, just after he'd learned the battle was taking place. In fact, he was probably watching from nearby, perhaps at the edge of the river. What should she do?

"Not water. . .leben!" she said in a low voice to herself, once the idea struck her like a bolt of lightning! Leben would put Sisera to sleep and then she could implement her plan.

Early that morning, Jael had prepared a batch of "leben," which is sour milk curds and yeast and looks much like cottage cheese. Her people felt this mixture had a medicinal effect, and that was just what she hoped for now. Carefully, she poured some of the leben into a magnificent looking bowl and then took it in to Sisera.

"I asked for water and you give me this elegant container of leben," Sisera said, smiling. He drank it all down and soon became very drowsy.

Then he said to her, "Stand in the doorway of the tent. If someone comes and inquires of you whether anyone is here, you are to say 'No.' "

She nodded her head in agreement, careful to keep her head low so that Sisera's eyes could not read the thoughts of her own. Trusting her, he reclined on the mat near the edge of one of the tent walls, not becoming at all suspicious. Jael gently covered him again with the mantle and walked away.

For some moments Jael struggled within herself, knowing what had to be done and attempting to gain the courage to take action. Once she was sure Sisera had finally drifted into a deep sleep, she went to Heber's wooden toolbox. There she lifted out his hammer and a long, iron tent peg. Holding them behind her back, she crept back to where Sisera lay snoring.

In one quick movement, she raised the hammer, put the tent peg to his head, and then hit the peg as hard as she could. It pierced right through Sisera's head and into the floor. His snoring stopped abruptly, and blood poured from the wound. Sisera, King Jabin's great general, was dead at the hands of a woman, just as Deborah had prophesied.

Jael shook with fright, knowing she had just killed this unsuspecting man. At that moment, it was difficult for her to understand that God had used her to stop this one who had attempted to destroy Israel's army.

Nauseated by the view of Sisera's body, she got up and walked outside, breathing the cool, fresh air that blew across the desert in the evening. She stared at the tall oak tree nearby, wondering what other secrets it had witnessed.

Barak, who had continued to pursue Sisera, came upon Jael, standing weak and pale outside her tent. Still dressed in his battle gear, she recognized him as Israel's general. Instinctively, she knew the reason he was there. "Come, and I will show you the man whom you are seeking," she said, and Barak entered the tent with her.

He stared in absolute disbelief at Sisera, lying on the ground with a tent peg driven into his temple. Quickly he looked around to see who else was there. *Surely, this woman couldn't have killed him!* he thought.

In a flash, Deborah's prophetic words came back to him. *The honor shall not be yours on the journey that you are about to take, for the Lord will sell Sisera into the hands of a woman.*

Instead of the exhilaration that Barak had anticipated experiencing, especially after such a great victory, he felt beaten, defeated, and humiliated. Deborah had warned him that God alone would have the victory in this battle, and yet Barak had selfishly sought glory for himself. After all, he'd been a former prisoner of the Canaanites when they had conquered Israel. It would have given him an incredible sense of vengeance to know that he had personally beaten them.

Looking at Sisera, however, Barak could not deny that Jael, who had sympathy for Israel's plight, had single-handedly managed to kill the king's general. "God could never allow Sisera to harm Israel," she offered in defense of what she'd done.

"Yes, I know," he responded without emotion. Then Barak instructed his men to drag Sisera's body out of Jael's tent.

At that moment, Barak felt small and worthless, as people

usually do when they've encountered one of God's awesome rescues, despite their pride, arrogance, and lack of worthiness. He knew in his heart that Deborah was not only ahead of him spiritually, but that she sought no glory for herself. Besides, if Deborah hadn't demanded that he take action on Mount Tabor, then he might have succumbed to the cowardice rooted deep within his heart.

Israel's soldiers had supported Barak in the battle, fighting valiantly despite the weather and being outnumbered, but in reality, they'd been following Deborah, whom they knew God had called to lead them. Now Barak silently walked away from Jael.

Once hidden from view of her tent, he sank to the ground in utter humiliation. His soldiers assumed he was praying for guidance. "God, forgive my unbelief and help me trust You."

CHAPTER 7

Deborah cleared the last of the rock formations and walked into a flat, grassy area as she made her way to the base of Mount Tabor. She purposely avoided looking at the carnage of war. Her tears had spilled out freely all the way down the mountain, but now she had to display strength and leadership before the small group of Israel's soldiers who approached her.

"Barak has found Sisera. He was killed by Heber's wife, Jael," she was told. Deborah said a silent prayer, knowing this death would weigh heavily on the conscience of any woman.

"Thank you for coming with the news. Where's Barak now?"

"He's gone after King Jabin," they answered.

So this long day isn't quite over, she thought, and then she prayed again for God's people, asking God to strengthen the people's will to obey Him. She only hoped that these descendants of Abraham, Isaac, and Jacob would understand the miracle that God had performed on their behalf this day. *And what of Barak?* Deborah wondered if he had learned from his formidable encounter with the Almighty.

Deborah's heart felt like a water glass ready to spill over with gratitude that had to be expressed. Joyously, she began leading the Israelites in a song about the wonders she'd seen. "The mountains quaked at the presence of the Lord, this Sinai, at the presence of the Lord, the God of Israel," she sang.

Although it was quite late now, and the moon cast glimmering light across the dusty road, all her neighbors and friends came out to meet Deborah as she neared her home. At the front of the group stood her husband, Lapidoth. Suddenly, he didn't care what the others thought as he ran to hug his wife. No endearing words escaped his lips, but Deborah knew from the tears he pressed against her shoulder that he cared deeply.

All of Israel celebrated that night, knowing their bondage had ended. God's mighty hand had freed His children once again. They feasted, sang, and danced. Who could sleep on a night like this?

Deborah wanted to hear all that had happened while her view of the battlefield had been obscured by the rain, wind, and hail. The women who had remained in the village also desired to learn everything that had taken place throughout the day. No one slept more than a few hours as they huddled by open campfires and shared the miracles God had wrought in their behalf.

One man told how the icy, cold wind had frozen the hands of the Canaanites so badly that they couldn't even get their swords out of the sheaths to use them. Because of this wind, many Israelites were undoubtedly kept from being wounded or killed. Sometime before dawn, they sang a final song of worship to their God.

"The stars fought from heaven, from their courses they fought against Sisera. The torrent Kishon swept them away, the ancient torrent, the torrent of Kishon. O my soul, march on with strength. Then the horses' hoofs beat from the dashing, the dashing of his valiant steeds."

What a glorious display of God's power they'd seen! This day would stand out in the memories of all those in Israel. Fathers would repeat it to sons for generations.

In yet another village was a mother who waited for a son who would never come home. Grief hung on her like a gown that's too large. "Sisera, oh, Sisera," she called to the night air, but no answer came.

She stood looking out the latticed window, the moon shimmering upon a road he would never travel again. What had become of the spoiler she'd made, the one that decorated the neckline of his robe? She'd embroidered it so lovingly with thread dyed a deep purple. Had the Israelites carried it off, along with the plunder of silver and gold from the war?

How could she comprehend how wrongly Sisera had acted toward Israel? For no matter what he'd done, he was still her son. In past battles with Israel, Sisera had been victorious. She had expected that he would be again. Now the king was gone, too. In one day her whole life had changed. She did not know the God who had protected Israel and therefore felt no hope for her future.

Deborah offered up a prayer for the Canaanite families who had buried their dead that day. Despite the fact that these people had chosen to be the enemy of God's people, she knew God still loved them. If only they could recognize Him as "Adonai," which was the Hebrew word for Lord. Wouldn't they realize the tremendous Power that had met their forces in battle? Surely as they analyzed the conflict, the rational conclusion to be reached was that a mere ten thousand troops did not repel the attack of an army the size of King Jabin's without a miracle of God.

Deborah was painfully aware that her people had been under Jabin's complete control for over twenty years. He had come out of a city called Hazor. His vast forces had been comprised of three hundred thousand foot soldiers, ten thousand horsemen, and over three thousand chariots. Sisera had been the commander of this vast army. As word of this devastating defeat spread throughout the region, perhaps it would serve as a warning to others who might consider controlling Israel.

Without their general, the remainder of King Jabin's meager forces fell into disarray and scattered. After his prayer, Barak finally realized that God would indeed fight for Israel. Bolstered by his faith in God's ability, Israel's general gathered his troops and headed for the city of Hazor.

As these warriors of Israel approached the city, men ran in fear for their lives while the women and children hid in their homes. News of the defeat had only provided a short time for them to take cover. Suddenly, those who had previously been friends of King Jabin separated themselves from him, lest they, too, might lose their lives.

Barak's troops seized this opportunity and overthrew the city to its very foundation. Then they thanked the powerful and true God of Israel Who had intervened to save His people in order to subdue their obstinate and ungrateful behavior. They knew the Lord desired that they understand the attitude that had brought about their control by other nations. Now Deborah wondered how God would help them turn all these years of disobedience around.

Before, men had consulted one another's opinions instead of following what they knew to be God's will. After the battle, Deborah returned to her duties as judge, and the people came to her with the most basic of questions, seemingly oblivious as to what God's laws meant. Long ago their Creator had presented Himself to Abraham as a "living God," speaking face-to-face with him. Deborah prayed that the Lord, Who displayed vital interest in a relationship with the Israelites, would show her how to reach the people with His truth.

Deborah could see that God's rescue of Israel had had a profound effect on Barak. The weakness that had permeated his character before had now been replaced with decisiveness and strength. Finally, he displayed that powerful and frightful aspect of the meaning of his name, "lightning," for when a man finally surrenders his spirit to God's control, his nature is changed from the inside out.

The fear Barak had formerly experienced had been due to the fact that he'd operated under his own power and assumed that the ultimate outcome of any event weighed solely on his shoulders. Now, relying on God, the burden appeared light. God's responsibility was to protect Israel, and Barak's duty was merely to follow directions.

The nations surrounding Israel no longer considered harming or attacking them. The outcome of Israel's battle with King Jabin had struck fear in the minds of their enemies. Neither could they forget about this victory when Deborah and Barak celebrated the event by continuously singing a commemorative song with the people of Israel. "Hear, O kings; give ear, O rulers! To the Lord, I will sing, I will sing praise to the Lord, the God of Israel. Lord, when Thou didst go out from Seir, when Thou didst march from the field of Edom, the earth quaked, the heavens also dripped, even the clouds dripped water. The mountains quaked at the presence of the Lord."

However, not all of the tribes of Israel had responded to the trumpet call for battle. In fact, some of them had not sent any representatives at all. Members of the tribe of Gilead had remained across the Jordan, while those in the tribe of Dan had stayed in ships, and men from the tribe of Asher had remained at the seashore. Had they been afraid of losing the battle? Or had they simply wanted to cling to their old way of life?

Deborah couldn't begin to know the intents of their hearts. Instead, she expressed gratitude for men like the ones of the tribe of Zebulun, who had showed no fear of death, for the healing needed by Israel had to be total. They couldn't afford to have warring factions from within their own nation. Perhaps personal shame in the face of this great victory would convict the men who hadn't fought with Israel.

Those who had been present at the battle had witnessed the power of God Almighty firsthand, but the tribes that hadn't been there had only heard the stories of the committed men who had. Would this secondhand information be enough to redirect their lives?

Deborah told and retold the battle accounts that Barak and his troops had lived through, and she taught the song to all who came and requested it, hoping it might stir in them the desire to get involved in the Lord's intervention for Israel.

"Most blessed of women is Jael, the wife of Heber the Kenite; Most blessed is she of women in the tent. He asked for water and she gave him milk, in a magnificent bowl she brought him curds." Over and over Deborah sang this verse of the song, enlightening all the tribes of Israel not only about the death of Sisera but also about God's fulfilled prophecy concerning its circumstances.

"Thus let all Thine enemies perish, O Lord; but let those who love Him be like the rising of the sun in its might." As Deborah continued the song, others joined in singing with her. Her aim focused on helping the Israelites to understand that the reason God had saved them was not because they had deserved it. The motivation had been His great love for them.

Sometimes Deborah viewed the Israelites like bad children wanting their own ways and refusing to respond to reason. Life appeared so simple to Deborah. She hated trouble and strife, so to avoid both, she chose to obey God's commands. When they had gone into battle, her stomach had felt like a tangled ball of string. Remembering how she had felt caused her to shudder, but as she released her apprehension, God replaced it with faith in His ability. Always better than to depend on human motivation before entering into challenging situations, Deborah prayed and trusted God. It wasn't that God's commands were easier for her than for others in Israel —perhaps in some respects they might have been even more difficult—but Deborah understood that God would never take her where He couldn't keep her. So she walked in step with Him.

Deborah knew she could not lead the Israelites unless she willingly followed God herself. Who would have believed that God could rescue them in the present unless Deborah had reminded them of the countless times He'd already intervened in their past?

Sometimes Deborah looked back to the time of her calling by God to be a prophetess and judge in Israel. Then she'd remember the flood of inadequacy and anxiety she had experienced. She had wondered how she could possibly meet the needs and demands of the Israelites. Expressing her feelings in prayer had always brought her back to rely on God's complete sufficiency and caused her to be content with her own position under His care.

Now she understood how to enable the Israelites to trust more. She would go back to the beginnings of His dealings with this nation and tell them everything. With renewed hope, Deborah arose from prayer, ready to begin her day.

From her vantage point high on the hill beneath her palm tree, Deborah looked out over the hillside and valley below. Dewy moisture covered the lush, tiered vineyards on the gentle slopes beneath her. Already men busied themselves hoeing and spading the land, careful to remove the largest stones (to use later for walls) to the back of each different level of freshly tilled earth. How carefully they prepared the land so that the ground would bountifully yield its sweet fruit. At times, one bunch of grapes could be so heavy that it needed to be carried on a pole by two men.

God had truly blessed their land, not only with many people but also with an abundance of crops. How tenderly He had cared for them, just as the vine dressers she now watched. *Yes, I can share this analogy with the people today,* she thought.

When Deborah spoke to the people, they responded immediately. Somehow in watching this process each year, they'd taken the whole thing for granted; but now, as Deborah spoke of how their loving God and Father prepared the soil of their hearts, tilled the ground around them, and even built a protective wall or hedge about them, it all became clear. He loved them and cared for them with perfect love. That's why they must give their obedience in return.

Now Deborah had laid a foundation on which she could

build even more of God's truths for them. She began to remind them of the things that God had directed Moses to write down. One important event involved man's first act of disobedience to God. It had happened way back in the garden of Eden. There had been only one tree in the whole lush paradise of which God had said Adam and Eve could not eat its fruit, and Satan, the evil serpent, had lied to Adam and Eve, telling them that God wouldn't punish their disobedience.

"Of course, once they had sinned God had to fulfill His warning: From that time on, man would die. This wasn't how God had wanted things at all. He had created man perfect and in God's image, and had asked only that man heed His warnings. Can you imagine," Deborah said, looking into the big brown eyes of one small, dark-haired boy, "Adam and Eve had everything and gave it all up, just to have their own way."

The small boy gasped, realizing that the first man and woman hadn't done any better than all the people he knew in Israel. All of them had disappointed God, too. He hung his head, feeling ashamed of himself, because he knew that sometimes he lied to keep from getting into trouble. He knew, too, that he fought with his brothers and sisters, rather than finding peaceful ways to solve his difficulties. A tear leaked out of the edge of his right eye and then his left.

Then Deborah reached out, extending her hand and pulling him onto her lap. As she dabbed at his eyes with the white cloth that had lined her lunch basket, she continued to teach the people. "But God loved this first man and woman so much that He didn't want to be separated from them, even though they had sinned. So right there in the garden, in front of the evil snake who had tempted them, God promised to send a Redeemer one day.

"And the Redeemer will be called the Messiah, for He shall save His people from their sins," Deborah said emphatically. The little boy smiled. Now he had hope.

"But how will the Messiah do this?" the little boy asked.

"Well, you know that we sacrifice a lamb each year as our people celebrate the Feast of Passover." The little boy nodded with understanding.

"Someday, God will sacrifice His own unblemished, perfect lamb, the Messiah, for all of our sins," she answered.

"Do you mean that this Messiah will have to die for me?" asked the small boy.

"Yes. That's exactly what I'm saying." Deborah looked into his eyes again. "And God will do this for all of us because He loves us," she added.

"Tell us more about the feasts," the people began to shout, suddenly eager to learn everything about the One who would bring them salvation.

"All the feasts point to different aspects of the Messiah's arrival," Deborah stated. "Let's start with the first month of the year, Nisan. You know that when God told Moses to take our people out of slavery in Egypt, He started what is called a 'holy convocation.' That means everyone in Israel is required to observe this feast. During the first Passover, the Israelites had to put the blood of the lamb on the doorpost so that when the angel of death passed by, he would not harm anyone in the house. Because the Egyptian Pharaoh refused to let God's people go, the firstborn of each household that did not have blood on the doorposts died.

"Each year, when you choose a lamb for your household, it is to be unblemished, or free of imperfections. Then you take the lamb into your home until it is time for him to be prepared for the meal." All the children nodded their heads, understanding what Deborah said, and knowing this was the best part of the feast for them, when they could play with the lamb.

"The second part of this feast takes place on the fifteenth day of Nisan, when your homes are cleansed of all the leaven, or yeast, which represents sin. Then a flat (or unleavened) bread is prepared so that we can remember the bread made in haste on Israel's night of deliverance from Egypt," Deborah told them.

"For seven days we eat this flat bread. On the day after the Sabbath, the priest offers a wave offering of a sheaf of barley, the first fruit of the harvest which has been planted." Deborah could hardly believe how attentively her people listened.

Now the children began to dance around in a circle in front of Deborah, excitedly anticipating the springtime celebration of Passover. Deborah smiled at their lighthearted fun, knowing that God had started these feasts not only to show Israel things about the Messiah, but also because He wanted them to observe joyfully the memory of these times in Israel's past.

Deborah stood up and stretched for a few moments. She'd been sitting on her straw mat for a very long time. Thinking the people probably wanted to go home, she hesitated before saying more. Then the children sat down again and the adults shouted, "Tell us more about the feasts, Judge Deborah!"

So she began again. "Well, as you know, our Sabbath is the day on which God said we are to honor Him each week, and the last day of the Passover celebration is a Sabbath. This day is called the celebration of 'Firstfruits.' "

"That's a funny name," said the little boy. "What does it mean?"

"These are the very first plants to come up after they've been planted in the ground," Deborah said, "and we offer these sheaves back to God because He is the One who has blessed us with a crop."

"Oh," said the boy, now that he understood.

When the children began to squirm, Deborah knew it was time to release them all to go home. It had been a long day, and she, too, was tired. As she stood to dismiss them, the little boy in front of her decided to ask one more question.

"Why does God want us to keep these feasts?" he asked.

His question impressed Deborah, because she thought it to be one that an adult might have expressed, and she couldn't help but smile at him. She placed her fingers on top of his curly dark locks of hair and tossed them about. "Because He wants us to remember Him and all the things He's done for our people," Deborah answered.

"Oh," said the boy, smiling back at Deborah.

Then without saying a word, he helped Deborah roll up her straw mat so that it could be carried home. (She never left it outside overnight because of the late evening and early morning dew on the ground.) Quietly, he slipped his hand into hers and walked with her down the hill and to the village. Since Deborah had no children of her own, she relished the sweetness of this moment. The boy's mother followed him and looked on approvingly, for who could be a better friend to him than Deborah, judge of Israel.

Once they reached Deborah's home, the little boy gave her a kiss good-bye and went on down the road with his mother. Lapidoth greeted Deborah. He had been outside their home watching the people descend from the hill and had been quite touched by seeing Deborah walking with the little boy. How he wished they had children. But perhaps if Deborah had been busy with her own little ones, she might never have had time to be the "mother of all Israel."

CHAPTER 10

As Deborah made her way to the hill and settled herself beneath her palm tree this morning, she saw a caravan of camels going across the desert. They headed eastward, toward the River Jordan. What strange and wonderful creatures they were.

Perhaps these camels had belonged to King Jabin. Deborah's brow raised thoughtfully, for the kings in this land used the animals for travel and also to transport their possessions. Now that he was dead, the wealth he had attained would fall into the hands of new owners. *How strange it is that people spend so much time acquiring things only to have them all left behind when they're gone,* she mused.

Deborah labored for her people, teaching them all she knew about the God Who had chosen her and now spoke His directions to her. How honored she felt, knowing that the way in which He directed her life made a difference for all the Israelites.

Lapidoth probably wished sometimes that God would have used him in such a mighty way, but he was content supporting all her efforts with the people. And he'd have been the first to defend her if anyone had implied that their roles in life might be reversed. God Himself had chosen Deborah, bestowing on her the gifts of a strong character and an obedient heart. These were the abilities that she offered back to

Him to use each day as she listened to the needs of her people. Her yielded heart became God's tool, and she was never fearful to tell the Israelites the truth about themselves or God's rules.

"Tell us more about the feasts," pleaded a group of children, seated at Deborah's feet.

Although the children had seen these celebrations each year, they wanted to understand the meaning behind each special day. How would they ever manage to obey Someone Whom they couldn't comprehend? These feasts told them so much about God and His expectations for them. Deborah knew that from the time she spent explaining things to them would come a whole generation of young people who would display an appreciation for God.

"Yesterday we talked about Passover. Who can remember what we said?" Several of the children showed they had listened attentively by giving an accurate account of what she'd previously taught them. Deborah's pride was obvious in the way she now looked at each of the children.

"One of the reasons God asked Moses and our people to observe these holy convocations is so that we will remain close to Him. Also, it shows the nations around us that the same God Who protects us with His power also desires to celebrate with us. We are unique in all the world, for it is from our nation that the Redeemer will come," Deborah said.

The wide-eyed children whispered, "Oh, we are very special."

"Yes, but we must remember that what makes us special is

the fact that God chose us. We can never think that we are different from other nations, apart from Him. It is His nearness to us that makes us a special people. That's why we hurt God so much when we disregard His laws and become disobedient like the nations who don't know Him at all. Can you see why it is so important to keep His commandments?" she asked.

"Another way in which the feasts help our people is to keep us together," continued Deborah. "You know there have been many times when other nations have tried to kill us or take us into captivity in faraway places, but when we obey God, He always brings us back here to our land," she added.

She had already taught the people about the Israelites being in Egypt for four hundred years and then God choosing Moses to lead them out of Pharaoh's control. This event had happened two hundred years before Deborah's lifetime, but the people of Israel had continued to recount the things that had happened to them long ago. By retelling these events to the children, history was passed on to another generation.

"We talked about how the Feast of Firstfruits is bringing back to God the grains that first appear on the land after planting. The next celebration is called 'Pentecost.' The word 'pente' means fifty, and at this feast the full harvest of crops has come in."

"How is this feast different from the other one?" asked the same little boy who had spoken the day before.

"During the feast of 'Firstfruits,' the priest offers the grains back to God upon the altar, but in this feast, the priest—who as you know comes from the tribe of Levi—takes two loaves of bread that are made from one lump of dough and waves them over the altar to thank God for the full harvest of grain."

"But I thought there was an animal sacrifice," said an older boy.

"Yes, that's right," Deborah answered. "God also told Moses to sacrifice one male goat for a sin offering and two male lambs one year old as a peace offering to Him.

"It's important for you to remember that with this feast there is a burnt offering, a sin offering, and a peace offering. Equally significant is the fact that it only takes place once the full harvest has come in from the fields of crops," said Deborah.

"Why does God always want things done a certain way?" questioned one young girl.

"Through our obedience to His commands, He is teaching us how to worship Him," said Deborah. "God doesn't need our food, but He does want us to be grateful for His gifts," she added.

"Why are there two loaves of bread?" questioned the older boy who had spoken before.

"Well, one represents Israel and the other is for those who are not of our nation. God loves everyone on the whole earth and desires that they come to know Him and love Him," Deborah responded, smiling at the children. "He wants each of us to feel His great love, so that we never think we are abandoned or alone in this big world," she assured.

"But we aren't alone. We have all the people in our village around us," said the young man.

"I'm glad you are safe and secure here," said Deborah, aware that he spoke with a child's heart. But many times she herself had experienced a sense of being completely alone. For example, when God had told her that He had picked Barak as the general to lead them into battle, she hadn't been able to talk with anyone about it. No matter how hard the times were, though, Deborah always understood that God cared for her and watched out for her. Now she hoped that she could adequately convey how the children might always know that God was guarding them, too.

During all the time that Israel had been preparing for the battle with the Canaanites, it had been mostly the adults who had prayed with Deborah. Once the children's fathers had returned from the battle, however, the children had begun discussing the great miracles that God had performed for the Israelites. Perhaps now the children also needed to know how to pray. Deborah had an idea.

"Do you remember when we talked about the first two people, Adam and Eve?" The children nodded their heads.

"Well, God used to talk to them as He walked in the garden in the cool of the day. He also gave them a chance to talk to Him. Now I know that you have watched me come up here early in the morning to pray, and your parents have prayed with me for Israel's deliverance. God heard our prayers and answered them, doing more than we had even hoped," she said.

"Judge Deborah, will you teach us to pray?" asked the children.

"Of course," she responded. "I kneel before God, because He is in control of everything and has made us and everything else in this world. So I owe Him worship," she said. Following her example, all the children knelt down, and Deborah led them in a prayer of gratitude to God.

CHAPTER 11

Now that Israel no longer experienced the bondage of the Canaanites, freedom filled the air as Deborah took time to notice the olive trees near her home. Some of these trees had been around since before Moses had lived, as they lasted for centuries. Deborah especially liked these trees in the fall of the year, when the blossoms from their dull, grayish foliage blew to the ground, covering it like a layer of snow.

Moses had spoken the truth when he'd written that Israel would have vineyards and olive trees that they did not plant. These trees were as ancient as the land God had given them.

Once the people had gathered beneath her palm tree, Deborah announced, "Today I will finish teaching you about the rest of the feasts." Quickly the crowd seated themselves on the grassy areas around her, and as usual, the children sat close to Deborah.

"Did you ever wonder why the trumpets are blown in Israel?" asked Deborah.

"When the battle started, men blew the trumpets," said the small boy who had sat on Deborah's lap several days before.

"That's right," she answered. "One of the times the trumpets are sounded is to call the men to war. God Himself is the one Who gave us this means of announcing important events to our people. Long ago, the Lord spoke to Moses and told him to make two trumpets of silver and use them for summoning the congregation of people.

"The trumpets are blown by the priests to announce the beginning of the feasts in Israel. When the people left Egypt, in the great Exodus, the trumpets sounded. The trumpets are also blown to sound the alarm in case there is trouble. God instructed us to do this so that all the people would be warned of impending problems. Many times this has saved us from our enemies. You see, the Lord has always watched out for us and shown us how to survive, no matter what has happened. Now let me explain the Feast of Trumpets," said Deborah.

"As you know, it begins on the first day of the seventh month, which is Tishri, and like all the other feasts, it is a day of rest. Our God knew that we would just keep working and never stop unless He instituted special days for us to relax. So all Israel gathers at the tent of meeting."

Once again the children listened patiently, with a desire to learn all of these customs that made their people different from other nations. The God of Creation spoke directly to their leaders, telling them of His desired actions.

"Now, on the tenth day of this same month, Tishri, there is another part of this feast, called the Day of Atonement, or Yom Kippur. This is the one day when the priest goes into the Holy Place to make atonement for all the sins that Israel has committed during the year. You already know that with all the idol worship and evil sacrifices to pagan gods, our people will have much to be sorry for this year. In fact, the mood of this feast is always very solemn and sad because we know how we have failed our holy and perfect God. Our sin is horrible in His sight. That's why He wants us to repent and start over each year."

As Deborah said these words, each person began to examine his own life, knowing how greatly he had failed to live up to the standards God held for His people. Guiltily they stared down at the dusty ground, ashamed for others to see their faces, as though their sins showed on the outside instead of the inside.

Recognizing how deeply wounded their spirits were, Deborah now began uplifting them by relating the events of the last part of this feast. "The third part of this celebration is called the Feast of Tabernacles. We live in tents or booths that we make for this occasion, so that we can remember how our people dwelled in tents as God brought them out of bondage in Egypt."

"Is that the time of year when we gather palm branches?" asked one older girl, attempting to keep all this information straight in her mind. Deborah nodded to affirm her answer.

"During the eight days in which we celebrate this feast, the priest offers a sacrifice of seventy bulls upon the altar. This is because God shed the blood of animals to cover the first sin man ever committed. The Lord told Moses exactly how many animals He wanted sacrificed during this feast," instructed Deborah. "These bulls represent all the nations of the world, as we know it, whom God wants to have converted to Him. That's why it is so important that we follow His laws," she encouraged.

"When the nations around us see how He protects those

who are obedient to Him, they will also want to know Him. Do you see now that we can reach out to those around us simply by doing what God wants?" Deborah asked, and the children nodded. How she loved to look into their dear faces.

"Why don't the people of other nations have to obey God?" asked a young man.

"Everyone has to obey God," answered Deborah. "It's just that many people choose to ignore Him, and when they do, the consequences are terrible. Just think about how King Jabin's entire army was wiped out in our recent battle. If King Jabin and his army had honored God by worshiping Him and keeping His laws, they wouldn't have been punished. We were also afflicted, through our slavery to the Canaanites. Finally, our people remembered the God they had tried to forget, and He came to fight our battle.

"Sometimes people think they can fool God by doing whatever they want," Deborah continued, "but God watches over us and knows the true content of our hearts. That's why it's so important that we stay close to Him and obey Him."

Another boy asked, "Why are the priests the only ones allowed to blow the trumpets?"

"God chose Aaron and his descendants, along with the men of the tribe of Levi, one of Jacob's twelve sons. They were dedicated by God to be in charge of everything that has to do with the worship of our God. Otherwise people might have been fighting over who should take charge of this important duty. Wouldn't it be terrible if people argued over how they are to honor our God?" prompted Deborah.

Those who listened to her day after day were constantly amazed at the way she could make such complicated things seem simple. Her questions always challenged them to think. How grateful they were that God had chosen her as judge over Israel.

As the sun sank lower in the sky, the trumpet blasts sounded, for the Friday evening Sabbath was about to begin. Deborah dismissed the people to go prepare their homes.

Each week the Israelites celebrated Sabbath, first by worshiping God and then by sharing a very special meal together with their families. Homes were decorated; small, low serving tables were neatly set, and even candles were lit. Then a cup of wine was blessed and distributed among the family members. The process was referred to as "Kiddush," which means sacrifice.

In the evenings, Deborah had been sewing a beautiful cloth for her serving table. Tonight she would drape it across the wooden tabletop and surprise Lapidoth. This simple act of weekly worship of God set them apart from all the nations around them, especially the Canaanites.

With the celebration of Sabbath, Deborah would share the meal with her husband. And a family who lived nearby would come to partake of the fine roast lamb, so that the house would be filled with joy. Deborah and Lapidoth, as well as all the Israelites, had much to celebrate this Sabbath. God had liberated them from oppression and now they were all beginning again.

Deborah climbed the hill toward her palm tree just as the sun peeked over the top of it. While she rolled out her straw mat, several of the older children, along with their parents, expressed a desire to pray with her. Now that she had taught them how to communicate with God, this desire had been planted in their hearts. His mercy was obvious to each of them, for when they'd been disobedient and had least deserved the Lord's help, He had protected them and spared their lives.

Deborah thanked the Lord for these people who now knelt in worship with her. She knew that all these young people would be needed to insure future stability for the Israelites. Their deep faith in God meant that someday, when they had grown up and started families of their own, the accounts of all that God had done for them would continue to be retold.

How could they keep silent after all they'd witnessed of God's power? With her eyes closed, Deborah reviewed in her mind the progression of events that had led to this moment. She remembered being in this very spot when God had spoken to her, revealing Barak as His choice to be Israel's general.

The people had prayed with her then, too, exhibiting great faith, despite the fact that she hadn't been able to relate any of the things God had told her. They had trusted God for a way through their oppression and pain, and He had not disappointed them. He never would.

A chill ran down Deborah's spine as she remembered not only the cold wind and rain upon Mount Tabor but also the awesome presence of God's mighty power at work. Thunder had boomed loudly, and then lightning had flashed in jagged streaks across the gray sky. She could still feel the very force of His angels as they had fought for the Israelites. Perhaps these scenes that had totally involved her senses would stay with her more vividly than if she'd been able to watch the battle with her own two dark brown, sparkling eyes.

What had it been like for the Israelites on the battlefront as the king's well-trained soldiers crumpled in confusion and then fell into the raging torrents of the river? Although she'd heard their stories, she could only imagine how it had felt to actually have been there.

Once the battle had ended and life had again appeared more routine and normal, this unusual phenomenon that the people had witnessed appeared similar to a dream, but as they spoke amongst themselves, the events again became real. And no one could dispute that God had intervened to save them all.

Now Deborah could hear a crowd gathering behind her. Another busy day had begun, and she would again teach Israel about the ways of the Lord. What a long way they had to go before they truly displayed the obedience within their nation that God deserved. There would always be some rebels who attempted to drag Israel back into the ways of pagan sacrifices and idolatry, just as there had been in the time of Moses; but the more that people understood about God, the less likely they were to follow these misguided rebels. What could a god of stone or wood, fashioned by their own hands, ever offer them compared to the love of the God of Israel?

Deborah realized she needed to relate again the laws that God had given to Moses, so she shared with the people these incredible events that had transpired upon another mountaintop, that of Mount Sinai.

"God had called Moses to this mountain saying, 'If you will indeed obey My voice and keep My covenant, then you shall be My own possession among all the peoples, for all the earth is Mine; and you shall be to Me a kingdom of priests and a holy nation.' They talked there of God's expectations for His people and then God gave Moses the two tablets of stone on which God had written with His own hand the commandments the people were to follow. But, as Moses descended the mountain, the people were dancing and worshiping a golden calf, and he smashed the tablets on the ground.

"Finally, the people repented of their great sin of idolatry, so the Lord called Moses back to the mountaintop. This time, however, Moses was instructed to cut out tablets of stone himself, like the first ones. After fasting for forty days and forty nights, the Lord again gave him the ten commandments upon the tablets, the words of the covenant that God made with Israel. He would be their God and the Israelites would be His people. Although God never forgot His part of the covenant, Israel repeatedly walked away from their commitment to Him."

Deborah now reminded her people why God wanted these commandments kept. " 'You shall thus observe My statutes, and keep My judgments, so as to carry them out, that you may live securely on the land. Then the land will yield its produce, so that you can eat your fill and live securely on it.' "

"Listen to these words God spoke," said Deborah. " 'I will make My dwelling among you, and My soul will not reject you. I will also walk among you and be your God, and you shall be My people. I am the Lord your God, Who brought you out of the land of Egypt so that you should not be their slaves, and I broke the bars of your yoke and made you walk erect.'

"Now, let us begin again to walk in obedience to God," Deborah encouraged, "so that we will never again be in bondage to an enemy of Israel. Out of this nation will come the Messiah, the Holy Son of God Who will walk among us and be the Passover Lamb Who dies to save His people from their sins."

All of Israel stood with Deborah that day, singing a song of praise to God. For forty years Deborah was Israel's judge, and Barak continued to lead Israel's army.

RUTH

THE WOMAN WHO LOVED

by Kjersti Hoff Baez

CHAPTER 1

The young woman cuddled the sleeping baby close to her heart. She stood at the edge of a meadow and sighed happily at the poppies blooming there. Bright reds and yellows swayed in the breeze in a blaze of color.

"Ruth!" someone called to the woman. "Let me take the baby. He should be inside sleeping, not outside like some miserable nomad." Naomi scooped the baby from Ruth's arms and smiled. "Besides, look at the sky! It's bound to rain."

The young woman glanced up at the sky and watched as clouds stumbled over one another in preparation for a storm. Naomi hurried into the house, but Ruth stayed behind. The breeze grew stronger, and the wildflowers bowed before the coming storm. As she lingered under the darkening sky, the storm's first raindrops tickled her face; and with their touch, Ruth remembered another day, another storm, and another place. . . .

Ruth lifted her face to the stormy sky and let the rain mingle with her tears. She felt lost, and her heart pounded with the realization that she would never see her young husband again. Mahlon was dead.

"Let's go home, Ruth." Naomi's voice was weary with grief as she turned to leave the tomb. A small cluster of women dressed in black followed after Naomi like a dark cloud. Their cries of mourning filled the air with sorrow.

Ruth stood for a moment, staring at the cave where her husband's body had been laid. "Home," she said to herself. The word that had once brought such happiness to Ruth now stabbed her with pain. She followed Naomi up the path and down the road to their house. The storm clouds darkened as if in sympathy with the young widow and the rain fell more fiercely on the rolling hills of Moab.

Ruth's sister-in-law, Orpah, met Naomi and Ruth at the door of their home. Her face was veiled in black and her eyes were dark with worry.

"It's Chilion. His fever is worse." Her voice trembled with fear. "It's just like Mahlon. He doesn't recognize me and. . ."

Naomi swept past her daughter-in-law and hurried to the corner of the room where Chilion lay on his mat. He tossed back and forth on the mat, groaning with pain. Naomi knelt beside him and grasped his hand.

"Chilion," she said desperately. "Try and be still. Everything is going to be all right."

Naomi's son looked up at her for a moment. He stared at her and trembled with fever. She searched her son's face for a flicker of recognition, but none came. He did not know who she was. Naomi rose to her feet with a sigh.

"He will be dead by tomorrow," she said quietly. "The Almighty has turned His hand against me." She tore at her mourning clothes. "I will wear sackcloth for the rest of my life."

The next day Chilion died. The men of the village came and buried him in his brother's tomb. Naomi's neighbors surrounded the three grieving women and shook their heads in dismay.

"Surely the gods are angry with you," cackled the voice of an old woman known as the Old One. "Perhaps you had better sacrifice to the mighty Chemosh, Naomi."

"Keep your gods to yourself," spat Naomi. "It is the Almighty Who has forsaken me."

"Well, I don't see what good your God has done for you," retorted the woman, her face puckered with wrinkles. "After all, first your husband and now both your sons are dead. So much for the power of Yahweh."

Naomi trembled with anger, but Ruth and Orpah gently pulled her away from the crowd. Together they trudged back to the house. Orpah pulled open the wooden door and followed Naomi inside. An oil lamp glimmered from its ledge in the wall, casting eerie shadows in the darkened room. Ruth stood frozen in the doorway, overwhelmed by the emptiness that glared out at her from the room that had been her home.

Ruth ran from the house and stumbled to the edge of a ridge, where she looked out at the highlands of Moab. The sun was making its faithful journey downward, leaving behind traces of splendor in red and orange. A mist hung over the mountains and Ruth gazed westward. Behind those hills lay Mahlon's homeland. As the sunset shimmered over Ruth's tears, she wondered if the glow of color would ever return to her life. She pulled her black sackcloth tighter and shivered in the coolness of the evening.

There had to be something more to life than sackcloth and sorrow. Ruth searched the horizon as if looking for a refuge, a place to hide. Something tugged at her heart, and for a moment she thought she heard someone call her name. Startled, she looked around but only caught a glimpse of an eagle as it flashed by on the way to its nest in the mountains.

Several weeks later, Naomi called her two daughters-in-law together and outlined her plan for them.

"Laban the merchant tells me the famine in Judah is over and that the Almighty has blessed His people with food. Our only hope is to journey to my home in Bethlehem. Perhaps we will be able to survive there."

"When do we leave?" asked Orpah.

"In three days Laban and some others are traveling to Judah. We will journey with them."

Naomi looked sadly at Ruth and Orpah. "I know it will be difficult for you to leave your homeland here. But what other choice do we have? No, my dear ones, we must leave this land of death. Go and say good-bye to your mothers."

She watched as Ruth and Orpah walked through the door into the afternoon sunlight and closed the door behind them. The ever-present oil lamp sputtered at her from its place in the wall.

"Perhaps," she muttered to herself, "I should never have left Judah in the first place."

CHAPTER 2

"You are a fool!" Ruth's mother hovered around her like an angry bird of prey. "You can't leave Moab with that woman. She's a Hebrew! The Hebrews hate us and the feeling is mutual. You will be miserable."

"She is my husband's mother."

"Your husband is dead."

Ruth said nothing, but the tears in her eyes spoke for her. Her mother's tone softened.

"Listen," she whispered. Her eyes darted furtively around the room as if there might be someone listening. "Perhaps the Old One is right. Perhaps you have angered Chemosh." Stepping back to the corner of the room, she picked up a small wooden cage and placed it in Ruth's hands.

"This is for you," she said. "Take it to the high place outside the village near the old almond tree. Offer it to Chemosh and beg for mercy."

Ruth looked into the cage at the small brown pigeon that cowered inside.

"It won't hurt to beg Baal, either." The fear and bondage in her mother's voice penetrated Ruth's heart with icy fingers. She felt her mother's arms around her and heard her whisper in her ear. "Go now. Offer it to the gods. Hurry."

Ruth hurried out the door and fairly flew to the high place. Several worshipers were there ahead of Ruth, and the pile of stones that served as an altar sizzled with blood and fire as they offered their sacrifices to the mighty Chemosh. The familiar chanting and wailing filled Ruth's ears and she shuddered. The chanting grew louder, and they motioned to Ruth to join them and make an offering. Suddenly, someone screamed. It was the Old One.

"Come!" she screamed at Ruth. "Come to the altar!"

Ruth nearly passed out with fear. The next thing she knew, she was running from the high place, hugging the cage to her chest. She stopped at a small clearing at the edge of a barley field. She gently drew the trembling bird from the cage and held it for a moment in her hands. Then she lifted it up to the sky and set it free. The pigeon's wings fluttered swiftly in the afternoon air, and Ruth watched as it escaped, a soft brown blur against the bright blue sky.

"I wish I could join you, little bird," the young widow whispered, watching until the pigeon disappeared. Then she turned toward the village. Her sad eyes could not see the poppies blooming by the edge of the road, nor could she hear the laughter of a little boy running in the fields nearby.

Two days later Naomi placed the last of their baskets on the back of one of Laban's donkeys.

"That donkey is fortunate that we are poor!" she said, gazing at the few baskets loaded on the animal. "He has only a light burden to carry!" She smiled at her two daughters-in-law and sighed. "If only my burdens were so light!"

"Eeyaah!" Laban's hoarse voice bellowed.

"We're off!" At his signal the small group of people and donkeys started their journey.

"Does the man have to yell?" Naomi groaned under her

breath. She motioned to Ruth and Orpah, and they fell into place behind the small group of travelers. "May the God of Israel at least grant us mercy on our way."

The early morning sun showered sparkle on the dew and Orpah gazed with longing at the fields that stretched out beside the road. Naomi watched her for a moment and then looked quickly away. Ruth looked straight ahead, her mind still numb with grief, and the screams of the Old One ringing in her ears.

They had not traveled far when Naomi stopped in the road and began to weep.

"I cannot do it," she cried. "I cannot do it."

Ruth and Orpah gathered around their mother-in-law and took her by the hand.

"What is the matter, Mother?" Orpah asked. "Why are you crying?"

Naomi shook her head. "It's no use," she sobbed. "I won't do this to you." She pointed back at their village. "Go back. Go back where you belong."

"What are you talking about, Mother?" Ruth's voice trembled.

"You must go back to the homes of your mothers. It would not be right for me to take you away from your homeland and your families. Go, my daughters. May the Lord be kind to you as you have been to me and to my sons."

She kissed them both and turned to leave them.

"No, Mother, no," the two young widows wept. "We'll go with you."

Naomi shook her head and looked sadly at their young faces.

"What do I have to offer you?" she asked. "Will I marry again and have two more sons for you to marry? And even if I did have two more sons, would you wait for them to grow up? No, my dears, you still have a chance for a good life here in your own country, with your own people. Go back. And may the Lord give you refuge in the home of another husband."

They wept all the more as Naomi begged them to return, but finally Orpah looked back at the village they had left behind. She kissed Naomi and Ruth good-bye, retrieved her basket from the donkey, and turned back toward the village. Naomi buried her face in her hands and sobbed.

"Surely the Almighty has set His hand against me," Naomi cried. "He has left me all alone." She looked up, fully expecting to be alone, but to her surprise Ruth still stood beside her in the road.

"What are you doing, Ruth?" she asked. She pointed to Orpah's figure hurrying toward the village. "See, Orpah is going back to her people and her gods. Why don't you go with her?"

Ruth clung to her mother-in-law. "Please don't tell me to leave you. Wherever you go, I will go, and where you stay, I will stay, too. Your people will be my people, and your God will be my own. Where you die, so will I, and there I will be laid to rest. May the Lord deal harshly with me if anything but death separates me from you."

Ruth's words touched Naomi's bitter heart, and a faint whisper of hope stirred within her. There was a stubborn look in Ruth's eyes; wordlessly, Naomi took her by the arm. Together they hurried to catch up with their fellow travelers.

CHAPTER 3

"So, have you made up your minds?" Laban shouted to Ruth and Naomi as they caught up with the caravan. "You've got to keep up or we'll leave you in the dust!"

Naomi glared at the merchant. "We can keep up. Just mind your own business."

Laban marched back to the two women, his eyes flashing. "This is my business. I have never once lost a man or animal on the trail, and I don't intend to start losing anyone now." He jerked his oily face close to Ruth and Naomi. "You know," he said, "there are bandits and wild beasts all over the wilderness. If you straggle behind, no telling what might happen." He looked to see if the women shuddered with fear. Naomi gave him a blank look.

"Besides," he continued, "I have a reputation that precedes me from Edom to Judah." Naomi glanced at his rather stout stomach.

"That's not all that precedes you," murmured Naomi.

"Don't say I did not warn you," Laban shouted as he stomped back to the front of the caravan.

"Do you think we will make it safely to Judah?" Ruth asked Naomi with fear in her voice.

"Don't worry." Naomi patted Ruth on the hand. "We'll be fine. Don't listen to that loudmouth Laban. He's just trying to scare us. Besides," she sighed and adjusted the black veil around her head, "could anything worse happen to us?"

Ruth said nothing, and they walked on together in silence. The morning sky shone blue and glorious about the small band of pilgrims. The young widow breathed in the cool air and let her thoughts wander over the last few days. She thought of Mahlon and how he used to smile at her and laugh at her auburn hair.

"Where did you get that hair?" he used to say. "You're supposed to have black hair like everybody else. You must be an angel."

Ruth blushed at the memory, and tears sprang quickly to her eyes. She hid her tears from Naomi and fixed her eyes on the dusty road at her feet.

I must be strong, she thought to herself. *I must be strong for Naomi.* She looked over at her mother-in-law. Naomi trudged along, her face creased with despair.

Ruth straightened her shoulders and tried not to feel so small beneath the widening sky. She caught glimpses of the desert to the east of the plateau on which they traveled. Flocks of sheep draped the hills like wisps of cotton, and once in awhile the faint whisper of a shepherd's flute teased the air with a hint of music.

Take a good look. The thought intruded on Ruth's mind. *You're leaving everything you've ever known. Your home, everything. Turn back now, while there's still time.* But a black wisp of smoke rising eerily from one of the high places smeared the sky, and Ruth knew she would never go back.

The morning coolness disappeared quickly, and the

afternoon sun warmed the faces of the travelers. Ruth was getting tired, and the glare of the sun threatened to put her to sleep. The monotony of their journey added to her weariness and she wondered when they were going to stop and rest. All at once the donkeys stopped moving forward.

"What now?" Laban yelled. He pulled at the lead donkey with no success. "At the rate we're going, we'll never reach Dibon before nightfall."

"So what are we going to do?" someone asked from among the group. Everyone started talking at once until Laban raised his hand for silence.

"Something is wrong," he whispered. "I can feel it."

In the momentary silence, everyone froze in anticipation. Suddenly, something darted across the road in front of the donkeys. It was a small deer. Everyone sighed with relief.

"Your donkeys are afraid of that?" someone said, laughing.

Their laughter was cut short. With a bellowing roar, a huge lion tore across the road in a streak of fury. It paid no attention to the frightened caravan but relentlessly pursued the frightened deer.

Ruth watched as the hunter and hunted disappeared into a distant ravine. The lion's roar swelled again, and in the silence that followed Ruth knew the tiny deer had lost its race for life.

"That was close!" Laban said, wiping his brow with his sleeve. "Good thing that lion didn't change his menu in the middle of his meal!" He laughed and slapped the dust from his sandals.

"Very funny," someone muttered.

"Oh, well," Laban continued. "A full lion is a happy lion. Let's get out of here. We'll be stopping at Dibon for the night. It won't be long now."

"Eeyaah!" Laban's voice echoed across the hills. "We are off!"

They reached Dibon just as the sun slipped behind the western hills. Laban directed Ruth and Naomi to the home of a fellow merchant.

"You'll have to sleep on the roof," Laban told them, "but that's better than sleeping on the ground, eh?"

The two women gratefully climbed the outer steps that led to the roof of the merchant's house.

"We'll be leaving first thing in the morning," Laban called up to them. "Be at the northern end of town by sunrise."

"Why don't you tell the whole neighborhood our business?" Naomi hissed at him from the top of the stairs.

"All right, all right," Laban lowered his voice. "Just be there on time." He spat on the ground. "Miserable old camel," he muttered under his breath.

Stubborn mule, Naomi thought to herself.

Naomi found two mats in a pile of baskets in the corner of the roof, and she gave one to Ruth. They unrolled the mats and lay down under the stars.

From the top of the roof, Ruth looked out at the town of Dibon. The whitewashed houses were cluttered together, and in the moonlight, they resembled a huddle of tired sheep. The excitement of being in a new place kept her awake.

"Tell me about your husband, Naomi," Ruth asked. "What was he like?"

Naomi sighed and closed her eyes. "Aren't you tired, Daughter?"

"No, not really. What was Elimelech like?"

"He was a good man," Naomi said, "but he was a worrier. He was a good farmer, but when the famine came, he panicked. And so we left Bethlehem and came to Moab."

Naomi sat up. "We weren't there long before he died." She looked at Ruth. "If he had lived, he never would have let his sons marry Moabite women. It is forbidden by our Law. Your gods are an abomination to the God of Israel."

Naomi lay back on her mat. "It doesn't matter now, though. Nothing really matters now."

Ruth said nothing and finally rested on her mat. The stars greeted her in silence, like glimmering guards of the night.

"It is forbidden." The words troubled Ruth, and she tried to escape them by falling asleep. But they followed her to her dreams. Ruth dreamed she was being chased by Elimelech. Elimelech turned into a lion and suddenly Ruth was a deer, running for her life. Then the Old One jumped out from behind a terebinth tree.

"Come to the altar," she screamed.

Ruth tried to get away, and an eagle flew by. She struggled to keep up with the eagle. "If I could only get to his nest, I'd be safe," she thought. "I'd be safe."

She woke up panting for breath. The lion, the eagle, and the Old One disappeared. Naomi slept quietly beside her and the stars still stood guard over the night. For Ruth, sleep would bring no rest.

CHAPTER 4

Before the sun was fully risen, Naomi and Ruth made their way to the northern end of Dibon. In the early morning light, Laban fussed and fumed over the animals, adjusting baskets and wineskins with extreme care. He stood back to survey his handiwork and greeted the two women with a smile.

"A fine morning for travel, don't you think?" he said, pointing to the clear sky with a sweep of his arms. "By the gods of Chemosh and Astarte, may we have a safe trip."

Naomi rolled her eyes and took her place at the end of the caravan.

"I thought Laban was a Hebrew," Ruth questioned Naomi.

"He is," Naomi replied. "But his faith depends on where he happens to be at the time. In Moab, he appeals to Chemosh for help. In Judah, he prays to the God of Abraham. I suppose if he lived in the Jordan River, he'd pray to the fish."

"Eeyaah!" Laban yelled, the donkeys moved forward, and day two of their journey began. Ruth was tired and thoughts of her nightmare from the night before preoccupied her mind. She wondered if the God of Abraham would accept her, now that she had claimed Naomi's God to be her own.

Laban joined the two widows and outlined the plan for the day.

"If all goes well, we will sleep tonight in the shadow of the great mountain of God. Nebo is a day's journey from here." He raised his arms dramatically to the sky. "May the God of Moses watch over us."

Naomi looked at Ruth and smirked.

"Such a man of faith," she said to Laban reverently.

The sturdy merchant blushed with pride and walked slowly back to the head of the troupe.

"Mount Nebo," Naomi explained, "is the mountain Moses climbed to get a glimpse of the land promised to the children of Israel. He was a great prophet of God. But surely Mahlon told you the story."

Ruth shook her head. Mahlon had never shared his faith with her; when she did ask questions, he would change the subject. She supposed now that he felt guilty about his marriage to her.

"The Lord used Moses to lead our people out of the bondage of Egypt into freedom. Moses talked to the Lord face-to-face."

Ruth could hardly believe her ears. "You mean he talked to God? Like you are talking to me?"

"Yes," said Naomi. She looked at her daughter-in-law. "Our God is not a stone image like the gods of your people. He is a living God."

She sighed and fingered her sackcloth. "The Almighty has turned against me. He has forgotten me."

Ruth put her arm around her mother-in-law and tried to comfort her. But her thoughts were of Moses, the man who talked with God. *Could such a thing really happen? Could men talk to God? Did He care about His people?* Ruth's heart raced with the possibility that these things might be true.

"Did he actually talk with God?" she asked Naomi. "Really?"

Naomi gave her daughter-in-law a stern look. "Of course he did. It is written that God spoke to Moses as a man would speak to his friend. Now don't trouble me with any more questions. You're wearing me out with all this talk."

With that, Naomi walked a little faster and left Ruth to walk alone, wrapped up in her thoughts. Overhead, a caravan of clouds crossed the sky like plumes of white as if to mimic the earthbound caravan that traveled slowly below.

Hidden from view behind the western hills lay the Salt Sea, and beyond the eastern mountains stretched a mighty desert. Laban skillfully led the donkeys on the narrow trails that went to Mount Nebo. In the afternoon, the mountain loomed into sight and Laban brought the caravan to a halt.

"Rest yourselves for awhile," Laban commanded the weary travelers. "We will arrive at Nebo this evening."

Ruth and Naomi sat down at the side of the road. Naomi handed Ruth a piece of bread and cheese and they refreshed themselves with water from their water pouch. The afternoon sun lent its gold to the mountains, transforming them with royal luster. Mount Nebo stood like a king in the distance. Ruth turned to ask Naomi another question about Moses, but her mother-in-law had closed her eyes to rest. Instead, she studied a busy harvester ant at her feet, struggling with a bit of cheese.

Laban's familiar yell spurred the group to continue their journey, and several hours later they arrived at the foot of

Mount Nebo. They set up camp in the shelter of a small ravine, and one of Laban's servants lit a small fire in the middle of their camp. The sun took back its gold from the mountains and left behind the purple and dark blues of evening.

Everyone gathered around the small fire and had their evening meal. Ruth and Naomi quietly enjoyed dried figs and raisins with their bread. Light from the fire flickered on the travelers' tanned faces.

Laban cleared his throat. "I have been to the highest ridge of this mountain," he said with a flourish. "I have seen what Moses saw when the Almighty showed him the Promised Land." He leaned forward, his face shining in the light and his dark eyes gleaming with excitement.

"When I was a young man," Laban began, "which wasn't so long ago, I might add, I came to. . ."

"Ayeeeee!"

His speech was interrupted by a scream. A black scorpion had darted out from beneath a rock near the fire. Before anyone could move, Laban grabbed his whip and, with a stinging slap of leather, killed it instantly.

The frightened onlookers stared at Laban with admiration. Even Naomi had to admit it was a spectacular display of skill.

"They only come out at nightfall," Laban explained, putting away his whip. "Now, where was I? Oh yes, I was a young man when I climbed Nebo.

"I made it to the highest ridge, to the top of Pisgah. It was a long and torturous climb," he spoke dramatically, "but I was strong as an ox."

"So what did you see?" one of the servants asked impatiently.

Ruth leaned forward in anticipation.

"What did I see?" Laban repeated the question. "What do you think I saw?"

"Oh, get on with it," Naomi muttered. "Hurry up so we can get some sleep."

Laban frowned at Naomi and continued with his story.

"As God is my witness, I saw what Moses saw. I saw the land of Canaan stretched out like a holy oasis. I saw the valley of the Jordan River, lush and green. I saw the shimmering green of the Salt Sea and the dusty haze of the mountains in the Negeb, where Abraham grazed his sheep. I saw the Sea of Kinnereth and the city Jericho. The mountains of Judea greeted my eyes. I saw it all."

Laban's words danced in the night air, and they swept Ruth away to the top of the mountain. She felt as though her eyes were seeing what Laban saw, what the great prophet Moses beheld when the Lord bade him climb and see the Promised Land. She fell asleep with Laban's words ringing in her ears.

The next morning the caravan left the shelter of the great mountain and headed for the plains of Moab. The bright green of the well-watered plains welcomed their eyes in the afternoon sun. As they approached the Jordan River Valley, Laban signaled the group to stop and rest.

"We'll camp here on the plains tonight and tomorrow we cross the river." Laban pointed to the land beyond the river. "The Promised Land," he said with pride. "May the God of Israel bless our journey into His land."

At the back of the caravan, Ruth laughed and turned to Naomi. "You were right," she chuckled, "Laban's faith changes with the wind!"

"Yes," Naomi replied. "And that is no faith at all."

They set up camp in the late afternoon and while Naomi rested, Ruth decided to explore the countryside.

"Don't go too far," Laban called after her.

From the top of a small hill, Ruth surveyed the southern end of the Jordan River and watched as it emptied into the Salt Sea. The emerald green of the river valley was a welcome relief to eyes weary of the dusty trail. Tall poplar trees graced the banks of the river, their shiny leaves dazzling like green gems in the sunlight. An occasional breeze stirred the leaves to dance and reveal their soft white undersides.

The mournful sound of a reed pipe called Ruth's attention

to a nearby hill. A flock of straggly sheep appeared and spilled over the top of the gentle slope. Their shepherd appeared soon after them, as straggly looking as his sheep. He spotted Ruth on the opposite hill and approached her slowly.

Ruth suddenly felt uneasy; her heart began to pound. She looked around behind her to see if she could spot the camp, but it was hidden from view.

The face of the shepherd darkened as he recognized Ruth's nationality.

He stopped and glared at her. "Moabite scum," he said with disgust. He spat angrily and leaned over to pick up a rock. "Why don't you go back where you came from?"

Ruth froze.

"I would be doing the Almighty One a favor by striking you dead." He raised the rock over his head. Ruth tried to scream, but no sound came out.

"And I would be doing the world a favor by getting rid of you." The crack of a whip pierced the air behind Ruth and she gasped with relief. It was Laban.

The shepherd lowered his rock and smirked at the stout merchant.

"I'm not afraid of you," he spat.

"That's because you're a fool." And with his whip, Laban struck the rock out of the man's hand with painful accuracy.

"Now get out of here before I shove your spit down your throat."

Ruth felt her knees give way and the edges of the air grew dark around her. She passed out and Laban grabbed her before she fell to the ground.

She came to as Laban offered her some water.

"It's all right now, he's gone," Laban spoke kindly to her.

Ruth sat up, still trembling with fear.

"Why," she whispered. "Why did he. . ." Her voice faded.

"He was a Hebrew, most likely a son of Gad. They settled in this area after the great exodus." Laban sat down on a large rock next to Ruth. "Before the Israelites crossed the Jordan into the Promised Land, they camped here, on the Plains of Moab. And Moabite women tricked some of the soldiers and leaders into worshiping their gods. This brought death into the camp."

Ruth sighed and looked out over the plains. She wondered how life in the Promised Land would be for a Moabite woman.

Laban seemed to read her mind. He looked down at the young widow and spoke quietly to her. "It's not going to be easy for you in Judea," he said. "You saw for yourself how that young fool of a shepherd acted."

Ruth trembled at the thought of what might have happened if Laban had not come along when he did.

"Thank you for helping me," she said. "You probably saved my life."

Laban laughed and shook his head. "Forget it." He stroked his beard. "Perhaps someone is looking out for you."

He got up and helped Ruth to her feet. "We had better get back to camp."

The setting sun stroked the Jordan River with flames of

color before it disappeared behind the distant hills of Judea. Ruth's shadow looked small beside Laban's large one, and she worried over the merchant's words of warning.

Naomi stood at the edge of the camp and greeted Laban and Ruth with a scowl. "Where have you been?" she demanded. She looked at Ruth. "I suppose you were wandering around the countryside, trying to get lost!" She stopped when she saw Ruth's pale face.

"What happened?"

"She almost got herself killed, that's what happened," Laban grunted. "You had better keep a closer watch on her, Naomi."

Naomi glared at the merchant and took Ruth by the hand. "It's time you got some rest, Daughter."

After they had eaten, Naomi insisted that Ruth tell her what was wrong. Reluctantly, Ruth told her mother-in-law about the cruel shepherd and Naomi gasped in horror.

"But Laban appeared out of nowhere and scared the man away," Ruth said quickly, "so everything is all right now."

Naomi shook her head. "Don't try to protect me, Ruth. You know everything is not all right."

Naomi looked southward toward Moab. "You should have listened to me and stayed with your own people. You would be safe there."

"Would I?" Ruth said, half to herself. She thought of the empty house, Mahlon's tomb, and the screaming of the Old One.

Naomi began to cry. "This never would have happened if

you had stayed with your own family."

Ruth put her arms around her. "You are my family now," said Ruth gently. "That is all that matters." She straightened her shoulders and lifted her head with a stubborn look on her face. "I made a promise and nothing is going to stop me from keeping it."

Naomi looked at Ruth and shook her head. "When you get that look, there's no arguing with you!" She gave her daughter-in-law a tired smile and lay down on her mat. "Try and get some sleep. Tomorrow we cross the river."

Beneath the velvet black sky, the tiny caravan rested. The camp's fire sparkled in the dark plain like a solitary star. Ruth tried to sleep, but the events of the day crowded her mind.

"Hello, old friends," she whispered to the stars. A few of them blinked down at her and Ruth smiled. "Do you know something I don't know?" she asked the night sky.

There was no answer, and Ruth turned and lay on her side. The memory of the shepherd's angry face came to Ruth and frightened her anew, but Laban's words returned to push away the fear.

"Perhaps Someone is looking out for you."

Those words flickered in the darkness of Ruth's sorrow and for a moment a tiny spark of faith stirred in the young widow's heart.

"Careful now, or you'll fall off the donkey!" Laban yelled at Naomi as she climbed up on the animal's back.

"Mind your own business!" Naomi yelled back at Laban.

"This is my. . ."

"I know, I know," Naomi shouted, "this is your business."

Ruth steadied the animal while Naomi settled herself on its sturdy back.

"I've ridden donkeys before," she muttered. "I wasn't always poor! Why, Elimelech had several donkeys when we left Bethlehem. But now everything has changed. I have nothing." Her eyes filled with tears. "If only my sons were returning with me to our home."

Ruth stood silently beside the donkey, struggling to hold back her own grief. She rested her hand upon her mother-in-law's arm to comfort Naomi and the older woman smiled through her tears.

"Dear Ruth!" Naomi sighed and patted her hand. "At least I have you!"

The Jordan River glistened in the morning sun and the poplar trees greeted the travelers with a canopy of green and white. A slight breeze whispered through the branches over-head and suddenly, quietly, it happened again. Ruth thought she heard someone call her name. A strange feeling swept over her, a feeling that this had happened once before. Ruth looked up at the dancing leaves, and then she remembered, it was the day Chilion died. She remembered climbing the ridge, grieving for Mahlon.

And there was an eagle, she thought to herself. *I remember I saw an eagle. . . .*

"Eeyaah!" Laban's yell interrupted Ruth's thoughts. "Get ready to cross the River Jordan!"

The donkeys moved forward and Ruth walked beside Naomi's mount. Her heart began to pound as she realized that as she crossed the river, she was crossing over to a new life. She was leaving Moab behind forever.

The water was almost waist deep, and Ruth got soaking wet crossing the Jordan. The smell of salt in the air drew Ruth's gaze southward toward the Salt Sea. Steep sandstone cliffs plunged sharply to the shoreline of the sea.

"That sea is dead, you know," Laban called back to his fellow travelers. "Not a bit of life in it! It's too bitter with salt."

Naomi looked toward the Salt Sea. "My heart feels like that," she said to herself. "Too bitter with sorrow to have any life."

As the group reached the other side of the river, Laban inspected the caravan and nodded with approval. "We're all here!" he said with satisfaction. "With the blessing of the Almighty, we will travel ten miles today."

Ruth wrung out the water in her clothes as well as she could. Naomi climbed down from the donkey and shook her head at her daughter-in-law.

"I told you to ride one of the donkeys!" she scolded Ruth.

"Now look at you!"

"I don't mind," Ruth smiled. "It will keep me cool."

"Ruth, sometimes I don't understand. . . ."

Naomi was interrupted by Laban's booming voice.

"See the mound over there? Near that grove of palm trees?" Laban pointed toward a clearing in the distance. "That is what used to be the city of Jericho. The city of palms," he said dramatically.

"You know the story of Joshua and Jericho, of course," Laban inquired of Ruth.

Ruth reluctantly shook her head no and Laban rolled his eyes and sighed.

"Well, I suppose I will have to tell you, Joshua was. . ."

"Oh no, you don't," protested Naomi. "It's time we got started. Forget the history lesson. Besides," Naomi said, "we paid for a trip to Bethlehem, not a guided tour of the Promised Land."

Laban stomped off and gave his customary yell to the donkeys. The wilderness of Judea loomed ahead of them, and its barren hills glared down at Laban's troupe. The heat of the sun settled heavily on the travelers, so Ruth's clothes dried quickly.

The trail led upward through the hills, and Ruth urged her mother-in-law to ride on the donkey. When Naomi reluctantly agreed, Ruth grabbed the halter of their donkey and brought it to a stop. After she helped Naomi climb onto the animal, they refreshed themselves with water from their supplies.

Ruth pulled on the halter so they could continue their

journey, but to her surprise, the donkey would not budge.

"Oh, no," groaned Ruth. "Laban's going to be so angry!" She watched as the rest of the caravan continued on without them. Ruth pulled harder on the halter and begged the donkey to move, but the animal just gazed at her with mournful brown eyes.

Naomi climbed off the animal, and together the two women urged the donkey to go.

"Forget it," Naomi said as she flopped down by the side of the trail. "It's not going anywhere. No doubt Laban has trained it well in the art of stubbornness." She sighed wearily and looked down the trail. The caravan had disappeared behind the edge of a hill.

"I'd better run ahead and get Laban," Ruth said.

"And I'll sit here and get ready for a long-winded lecture."

Ruth hurried up the trail; as she reached the bend in the road, she almost ran into someone.

"Now what?" Laban shouted. Ruth stood before him like a forlorn child.

"The donkey won't move. We tried everything but. . ."

"I turn my back for one minute and you two disappear into thin air!" He marched down the road and Ruth chased after him, apologizing all the way.

Naomi sat by the side of the road, arms folded. Laban came to a halt in front of the donkey and glared at the two women.

"Who stopped the donkey?" he asked. "No one is to stop the donkeys except me. Who stopped the donkey?"

"Well, I did," Ruth said softly, "I was only trying. . ."

"Never mind!" Laban growled. "Don't you know. . ."

"Here we go," Naomi said.

"Don't you know it is dangerous to be left alone in the wilderness? There are wild animals in the hills, leopards and bears, not to mention the fierce ones that walk on two legs."

"I'm sorry," Ruth said. "I won't. . ."

"Furthermore, I am in charge of this trip, and I have never lost a man or animal on the trail. I don't intend to start losing anyone now."

"We know," Naomi replied. "We know. Now, can we go?"

Ruth helped Naomi get back on the donkey, and Laban walked ahead of them. He looked back at the two women, who smiled cheerfully at him.

"Just don't let it happen again!" He frowned and let out a yell. "Eeyaah!"

The donkey moved immediately and followed his master up the trail. They joined the waiting caravan and continued their journey in the bright afternoon sun. Ruth gazed at the hills and the Judean sky. She caught a glimpse of several gazelles bounding over the high places, their pale brown fur blending in the color of the hills. On another ridge, wild black goats stood motionless, like a silent cluster of mourners on the barren heights.

As she observed these scenes, Ruth tried to imagine that Mahlon's eyes had seen the same things when he traveled to Moab but thoughts of her husband only renewed her grief, and with every step she took, Ruth wondered if the pain would ever go away.

CHAPTER 7

The night passed quickly in the Judean wilderness. Ruth and Naomi slept in the shelter of a small cave near the camp. When the first rays of morning streaked the sky with light, Laban had everyone up and ready to go.

"It is only ten miles to Bethlehem," he told them. "I expect to make good time and arrive there this afternoon," he continued, "if everyone cooperates." He glared at Ruth and Naomi. "Try and keep out of trouble."

Ruth blushed, but Naomi returned his glare. The fresh morning air was bright with the promise of a clear day. The caravan continued its upward climb toward the plateau where Bethlehem was located. The rocky hills crowded the trail like somber spectators watching silently as the little band of people made its way through the wilderness.

Something in the sky caught Ruth's eye and she squinted, trying to get a better look.

Suspended high in the air, barely moving in the sapphire blue sky, several large black birds hovered.

"Vultures," Laban called back in a matter-of-fact voice. "Messengers of death."

Ruth looked at the scavengers soaring overhead. She shuddered but couldn't take her eyes off them.

"They're probably looking for me," Naomi said. "Unfortunately for them, I'm still breathing."

Ruth looked at her mother-in-law.

"Don't say such things," Ruth scolded her mother-in-law. "You mustn't talk like that."

Naomi shrugged her shoulders and shifted her sackcloth.

Suddenly, the vultures dropped swiftly to the earth, just beyond a nearby hill. Ruth closed her eyes for a moment and steadied herself against the donkey.

I'm so tired, she thought to herself.

"Feeding time!" Laban yelled. The caravan came to a halt and Laban sauntered to the back of the caravan, inspecting the donkeys as he came.

"We might as well join the vultures and eat now, too." He laughed and slapped his ample sides. "We'll take a short break and be on our way. It won't be long now."

Naomi climbed off the donkey, and the two women sat together by the side of the road and ate their cheese and dried figs.

"This is the last of it," Ruth said, holding up the small, empty basket. She handed her mother-in-law the last piece of cheese. "You'll need your strength for the rest of the journey."

Naomi hesitated, but Ruth had that stubborn look on her face, so she gratefully accepted the cheese. Ruth smiled and gave her mother-in-law a gentle pat on the arm. "Once we get to Bethlehem, we'll be able to get more food."

Naomi's face was etched with worry. "I'm not so sure about that," she said doubtfully.

The heat of the afternoon sun wrapped itself around the little caravan as they made their way to the edge of the wilderness. At times the road looked hazy in the glare, and the air shimmered like liquid light on the road before them. Finally the travelers left the desolation of the wilderness behind them. The green hills of central Judah filled their eyes, and a cool breeze filtered down from the plateau.

"We're almost there!" Laban shouted back to his weary followers.

Ruth's heartbeat began to race at the thought of approaching Bethlehem. *My new home,* she thought.

"It's just beyond this hill," Laban yelled.

"All right, all right, so why don't you announce it to the whole world," Naomi muttered under her breath. She began to tremble as they climbed the sloping hill. "Oh, Elimelech, Elimelech," she whispered. "I've come back to our home with empty arms."

The road widened as they reached the top of the hill. Beyond the fields of ripening grain lay the village of Bethlehem.

"There she is!" shouted Laban. "There she is!"

The sandy-colored mudbrick houses sat close together on the top of a ridge. Here and there whitewashed houses gleamed in the afternoon sun like occasional bright teeth among the faded tan ones. Ruth looked across the fields at Bethlehem and her heart skipped a beat. Her new life was about to begin.

Naomi stifled a sob and stopped in the middle of the road. Ruth quickly put her arms around her mother-in-law.

"I don't think I can bear it," she cried. She clung to Ruth and wept bitterly. "I don't think I can stand to go home alone like this."

"But you're not alone," Ruth implored Naomi. "I'm here. I'll help you."

Naomi smiled sadly at Ruth. "I know, but still. . ."

Ruth looked down at her dusty feet and spoke softly to her mother-in-law.

"I know I'm not Mahlon or Chilion, but I do love you." Her chin trembled, but she looked Naomi straight in the eye. "I know I can help take care of you."

Naomi wiped the tears from her eyes. She studied her daughter-in-law's face. She wondered to herself where such love came from.

"Let us go," Naomi said finally, "before Laban starts yelling."

Together they caught up with the caravan as they made their way toward the village. Ripened fields of barley and almost-ripened wheat fringed the sides of the road in abundance.

"What did I tell you?" Laban walked back to Naomi and Ruth. "The famine is over! The Almighty has blessed His people with food!"

Naomi nodded in agreement. "It's true. Look at those fields!"

"This is the beginning of the barley harvest," Laban instructed Ruth. "After that, the wheat should be ready."

Ruth listened as Laban gave a detailed history of the harvest.

"And you know, there is provision in the words of the Lord for the poor and the. . .uh. . ." He looked at Ruth. "And the alien." He cleared his throat importantly. "The poor and the alien may glean the field after it is harvested. Crops on the edges of the field are to be left for the poor also."

"What he means, dear Ruth," Naomi snorted, "is that we get the leftovers." Naomi strode past Laban in a huff.

Laban turned to Ruth. "She's a proud woman, Naomi is," he said, "but pride can starve you. My advice to you is to accept the kind provision of the Lord."

Ruth nodded and as Laban walked away, a quiet peace fell softly on Ruth like a finely woven shawl. "The provision of the Lord," she whispered to herself. She looked toward Bethlehem with new hope ringing in her heart.

Before the group reached the gate of the village, a flock of little children ran out to greet the caravan. They whooped with excitement when they saw who it was.

"It's Laban!" they shouted. "Laban, Laban, big as a boat! Laban, Laban, mean as a goat!" They swooped down on Laban and surrounded him. He laughed and shooed them away.

"Out of my way!" he yelled, waving his arms. "Out of my way or no surprises for you!" At that, the children respectfully made way for Laban and his donkeys.

Several men and women came out to welcome the travelers. Naomi pulled her sackcloth close and walked toward the gate. She paused only for a moment at the gate where her husband had once sat as an elder of the village. As she continued on, the women stared at her.

"Why, that looks like Naomi," one of them whispered.

"No, that can't be she. She looks so old!"

"Yes, it is Naomi," one of the older women chimed in. "I ought to know! We were neighbors!"

"Naomi!" The woman called after her, and Naomi stopped to face her.

"Hello, Hannah," Naomi said.

"I knew it was you, Naomi."

"Yes, it's I, but don't call me Naomi. Call me Mara, because the Almighty has filled my life with bitterness. I left

Bethlehem with my arms full with my family, but now the Lord has led me back with empty arms." She turned away and walked through the gate.

"But Naomi. . ."

"Why should you call me Naomi? Doesn't that mean 'pleasant'? No, Hannah, my name is Mara now."

As Naomi walked away, the villagers crowded around Hannah, thirsting to hear the news. What had happened to Naomi? She was wearing sackcloth! What happened to Elimelech and the two boys?

"I don't know," said Hannah, shaking her head. She watched Naomi's stooped figure trudge slowly toward her old home. "But it looks like she's lost everything."

Ruth waited patiently while Laban untied their few belongings from the donkey's sturdy back. He handed her their mats and baskets.

"Can you carry all that? The house isn't too far."

"I can manage," Ruth replied. "Thank you for your kindness." She smiled. "And your stories."

Laban blushed and grinned at Ruth. "You're welcome, young lady! You're a good listener!" Laban looked around for Naomi. "You'd better catch up with your mother-in-law."

"Yes, I will, and thanks again." Ruth headed in Naomi's direction.

"And Ruth!" Laban called to her and motioned toward the crowd gathered at the gate. "Be careful; some people's words may be sharper than that shepherd's stone."

Ruth nodded and hurried past the villagers. "Naomi!"

she called to her mother-in-law. "Wait for me!"

The women watched as the young woman rushed by.

"Well, who do you suppose that is?" Hannah wondered.

"Why, she's from Moab!" gasped a woman named Judith.

"Maybe she is Naomi's servant," suggested one of the ladies.

"I doubt it," Hannah replied. "By the looks of things, I doubt Naomi would have a servant!"

"You don't suppose. . ."

"Her daughter-in-law!" Judith fairly shrieked. "I say she's Naomi's daughter-in-law!"

All the women began to talk at once. It couldn't possibly be! It wasn't right for a Hebrew to marry an idol worshipper. What a scandal!

Hannah gathered her shawl about her and approached Laban. He was tending his donkeys in front of an admiring audience of children.

"Welcome back, Laban," Hannah said with a friendly voice. "How was your journey?" Hannah cleared her throat. "Did you make good time?"

"Four nights, five days. The usual." Laban pulled at his black beard. "What is it you really want to know, Hannah?"

The woman didn't hesitate for a moment.

"Who is that young woman with Naomi?"

"Oh, so that's it." Laban spat into the dust. "I figured as much."

"Well, who is she? She looks like a Moabitess."

Laban turned back to his donkeys. "She is," he said tersely.

"Why is she with Naomi?"

Laban struggled with a stubborn knot on one of the halters. Hannah hurried around the donkey and faced the sturdy merchant.

"Well, Laban, who is she?"

"She's Naomi's daughter-in-law!" Laban shouted at Hannah. She jumped back in surprise.

"I knew it!" chortled Judith triumphantly. "I knew it. It's a disgrace," she added in religious tones.

Laban turned abruptly away from the women, making it clear the subject was closed. "Old hens!" he mumbled under his breath.

While the crowd boiled over with the news, Ruth caught up with Naomi and followed her to their home. It was at the edge of the village, overlooking the terraced fields of grain. Naomi stopped and stared gloomily at her old house. The whitewash had long since faded away, and the door had rotted to pieces. A family of goats had taken up residence inside.

Ruth hurried in and herded the reluctant goats out the door. She quickly swept the clay floor and laid out Naomi's mat so she could rest. Naomi collapsed onto her mat and cried herself to sleep.

The young widow busily finished cleaning the house and setting it in order. She carefully retrieved their only oil lamp from one of the baskets and placed it on the ledge in the wall. Ruth poured some olive oil into the clay lamp and lit it.

The familiar sputtering of the lamp and its warm glow comforted Ruth and made her feel at home. She looked around the room and tried to imagine Mahlon as a young child, running in and out the door. But the room was empty, except for her sleeping mother-in-law, and suddenly Ruth realized once and for all that Mahlon was gone.

She walked through the door and looked out over the fields of grain. In her mind's eye she looked past the wilderness, past the Salt Sea, and into the land of Moab. "Goodbye, Mahlon," she whispered. Ruth let go of him, and peace filled her heart.

Evening was drawing near, and the fields caught fire with the golden-rose color of the setting sun. Ruth breathed a prayer of new beginnings to the Almighty, and as an evening breeze caressed the ripening grain, Ruth knew in her heart the Lord had not deserted them.

The next morning the sharp pains of hunger wakened Ruth from her sleep. Naomi was already up, standing at the open doorway.

"Good morning, Daughter," Naomi said. "How did you sleep your first night in Bethlehem?"

"Very well," Ruth replied. "It's so peaceful here."

"Yes, it is a quiet place." Naomi looked with concern at her young daughter-in-law. "You look a little pale, my dear."

"I'm fine." Ruth rose from her mat and rolled it up. She sat it in the corner next to Naomi's. "I'm just a little hungry, that's all."

Naomi frowned and shook her head. "Just a little? I know better than that, my dear. We haven't eaten since yesterday afternoon." She looked at their empty baskets. "I'm afraid we have no food."

"If you let me, I would like to go to the nearby fields and gather up the leftover grain. Laban said. . ."

"I know what Laban said," Naomi retorted. Her tone softened and she put her arm around Ruth. "I can't believe it has come to this."

"I'll go at once," Ruth said eagerly. "Perhaps I will find favor with one of the workers and they'll let me glean in their field."

"All right," Naomi agreed. "After all, we really don't have a choice."

Ruth pulled her shawl around her shoulders and hurried out the door. "Be careful!" Naomi called after her.

Naomi stepped outside the door and looked around the familiar neighborhood. Despite all the hardship, she was glad to be home. There were some new houses alongside the old ones, but for the most part nothing had changed.

Nothing except me, she thought. *I used to be so happy, so full of life. And now. . .*

"Naomi!" A voice called to her from the next house. It was Hannah.

Hannah walked quickly toward Naomi's house and greeted her with a hug.

"Let me get a good look at you," she said kindly. "I didn't get a chance to talk to you yesterday. After all, you'd just come back and you were tired of course, and. . ."

"Hannah," interrupted Naomi, "would you like to come in and sit down?"

"Of course!" She followed Naomi into the house. They sat down on the flat stones near the empty fire pit that was used for cooking. The lonely oil lamp flickered bravely on its ledge, illuminating the small room.

"Naomi. . ." Hannah hesitated. "Naomi, what happened?"

"Soon after we moved to Moab, Elimelech became ill and died. After his death, the boys married two Moabite women."

"Oh no!" Hannah's hand flew to her mouth. "I mean, after all, it is forbidden. . . ."

"Orpah and Ruth were very kind to my sons." Naomi's eyes were flashing with anger.

"Mahlon and Chilion did as they pleased after their father died. What was I supposed to do?"

"Now, now my dear, I did not come here to get you all upset."

"Then what did you come here for?" Naomi demanded.

Hannah's face reddened. "I just came to see how you were and find out what happened. . . ."

"That's nice," Naomi said sarcastically. "Now be sure everyone in the village gets the news." She pointed to the corners of the almost-empty house. "Don't forget to say we're as poor as beggars."

Naomi's embarrassed neighbor got up quickly and hurried to the door. She paused for a moment and looked at her old friend sitting alone on the floor. "I'm sorry," Hannah whispered. Then she was gone.

Naomi covered her face with her hands and wept bitterly.

The cheerful morning sunlight matched the singing in Ruth's heart as she walked down the road toward the barley fields. Today she would bring home food for her mother-in-law.

"It's in the word of the Lord," she reminded herself. "The foreigners and the widows can pick up the leftovers." She quickened her pace and looked out over the numerous fields of grain. Soon she came upon a barley field where the harvesters had already begun their day's work. Ruth approached the foreman of the workers.

"May I please glean behind the harvesters in your field?"

The foreman eyed Ruth and frowned. "Who are you?"

"I am Naomi's daughter-in-law," she said firmly. "I am from Moab."

The man hesitated and then shrugged his shoulders. "All right," he said. "But stay well behind my workers and don't make any trouble. I'll be watching you!"

Ruth bowed her thanks and took her place behind the harvesters. The young men were busily cutting through armfuls of barley with their sickles. The women followed behind them, binding the armfuls of grain into neat bundles. Ruth drew open her shawl and began to pick up the leftover stalks.

Occasionally, the workers looked back at the newcomer gleaning behind them. Ruth could hear them talking among themselves, but she worked steadily on, ignoring their stares. The sun shone hotly on the open fields and after several hours of exhausting work, Ruth rested beneath the workers' shelter.

"Why didn't you stay in Moab, where you belong?" The sharp words startled Ruth and she turned to face the accusing voice. It was Judith. "We don't need you or your filthy gods in Judah."

Ruth felt her anger boil up inside and threaten to spill out in fierce words, but a calm voice from the other side of the shelter intervened.

"Leave her alone, Judith. The poor girl's got enough troubles without you adding to it." A woman Ruth's age sat down next to her. "My name's Abigail," she said with a smile.

"My name is Ruth," the young widow replied gratefully. "How did you know about me?"

"Laban's my uncle," said Abigail, "and he loves to talk."

Ruth started to laugh, but Judith gave her a harsh look.

"I'd better get back to work."

Ruth turned her back on the turmoil in the shelter and returned to her hard labor under the sun. Her heart ached at the thought of Judith's words. She had left the gods of Moab behind in her homeland. Naomi's God was her God now; couldn't anyone see that?

A strong deep voice interrupted Ruth's thoughts.

"The Lord be with you," a man called to the workers.

"The Lord bless you!" they hailed back to him. The man noticed the newcomer in the field and smiled at her. Ruth wondered who the tall man was and watched him as he approached the foreman.

"That's Boaz, the man who owns these fields." Abigail stood at Ruth's side. "He's an important man in Bethlehem."

Boaz joined his foreman and looked out over his fields and workers.

"Seth, how is the harvesting going today?"

"Very well, Boaz. We've had no trouble today."

"Caleb's fields were raided last night. Better keep your eyes open."

"Will do."

The young stranger with auburn hair caught Boaz's attention.

"Who does that young woman belong to, Seth?"

"That's the Moabitess that came back with Naomi. She asked if she could glean and she's been working hard all day." Seth folded his arms and watched as Ruth continued to gather the fallen grain. "She only rested once in the shelter. Thought she might give us some trouble, but so far. . ."

"See to it that none of the men trouble her!" Boaz strode over to the men and gave them clear instructions. Then he approached Ruth and called her to his side.

"Listen, Daughter," he said quietly to the young woman. "Stay in my fields to glean. Follow my servant girls and watch where the young men are harvesting. Those are my fields and you may glean as much as you like." He smiled down at Ruth. "I've told my men not to harm you and you can drink from the waterskins as often as you wish."

Ruth stared up into the face of the kind man. His brown hair and beard were speckled here and there with gray and his warm brown eyes sparkled with life. His face was tan from the sun and when he smiled, the tiny wrinkles near his eyes smiled, too.

She knelt and bowed before him. "Why do you give me such favor? I am a Moabite. Why should you notice me?"

"I've heard all about you," he said. He took her by the hand and helped her to her feet.

"I know that after your husband died, you came here with your mother-in-law. You've left your home and family and come to live in a land you've never seen before. All because you care about Naomi. May the Lord bless you for what you have done. May you be fully repaid by the Lord, the God of

Israel, under whose wings you have found a hiding place!"

Boaz's words ignited Ruth's newborn faith and it burned brightly in her heart. "You are very kind, Sir." Ruth's voice trembled. "Your words bring me great comfort. I hope I can continue to find favor in your sight."

Boaz pulled a stalk of barley and fingered it gently.

"Generally, a farmer gets what he planted. You planted seeds of sacrifice and love. And I know you will reap a bountiful harvest."

Boaz looked up at the sun and called out to the workers.

"Time for the midday meal!" He motioned to Ruth to join them and he gave her some roasted grain to eat. He offered her the wine vinegar to dip it in and Ruth's strength was renewed. Boaz gave her so much grain that she put some aside for Naomi.

When Ruth got up again to glean, Boaz gave his men more instructions.

"Let her glean among the sheaves, and pull out stalks for her to gather. And don't give her a hard time about it."

The workers looked at Ruth with new eyes after Boaz arrived. And Judith kept her mouth shut for the rest of the day.

Ruth worked in the field until evening came. Then she threshed the grain and scooped the kernels of barley into her shawl. When she arrived home, Naomi was waiting for her at the door.

CHAPTER 10

"I was worried sick about you!" Naomi pulled Ruth into the house and sat her down on her mat. "How did everything go?"

Ruth opened her shawl and poured its contents into one of the baskets. Naomi's eyes opened wide as she watched the grain fill the basket to the brim. She looked at her daughter-in-law with amazement.

"Where in the world did you glean today?"

Ruth's face was flushed with color from her hard day's work. She handed Naomi the roasted barley she had left over from the midday meal. "I worked in the fields belonging to a man named Boaz. He was very kind to me."

"I can see that," Naomi said in astonishment. "I can't believe the amount of grain you gathered! May the Lord bless that man for being so good to you!"

Ruth smiled and lay down on the mat. "He told me to glean in his fields for the rest of the harvest."

Naomi's heart was stirred with renewed hope. She looked at the abundant food and at her loving daughter-in-law. "The Lord has not forgotten us," she said. "I can see that His kindness toward us has not stopped."

Ruth nodded with joy at hearing Naomi's words. It was so good to hear happiness in her mother-in-law's voice again.

"Boaz," Naomi said his name thoughtfully. "Why, Boaz is a close relative of my husband! He might be able to help us."

"He told me to stay with his workers," Ruth repeated sleepily.

"That's a good idea, my dear. If you stay with his servant girls, then no one will hurt you."

Naomi's words lulled Ruth to sleep and all was quiet in Bethlehem. Naomi sat up late into the night, watching her tired daughter-in-law sleep. The ever-burning oil lamp cast a glow on the mud brick walls and Naomi's heart warmed with the knowledge that God had been with them all along.

The days of the barley harvest passed quickly. Every morning Ruth walked the dusty road to the fields of Boaz and joined his maidservants there. She worked steadily each day while Naomi took care of the cooking and cleaning. The townspeople kept an eye on the Moabitess and took note of her hard work and devotion to Naomi.

"She can't be all that bad," one of the women whispered as Ruth passed by the well in the center of the village. "She certainly takes good care of Naomi. Poor thing. She must be homesick."

Hannah nodded in agreement. "Poor thing. And I must say, she loves Naomi like she was her own mother!"

"I don't trust her!" grunted Judith. "After all, she's from Moab!" She signaled to the other women to draw closer. "I bet she sneaks off at night and worships that horrible god Chemosh."

The women broke into feverish whispering. Suddenly, the snap of a whip crackled in the morning air and startled the busy group into silence.

"Laban! Why, Laban, son of Jacob, you scared us half to death!" Hannah scolded the portly merchant.

"Oh, I am sorry, ladies." Laban bowed graciously. "I was just practicing. I heard there were vipers near the well that needed tending to."

"Uncle Laban!" Abigail laughed. "You are terrible."

Judith picked up her water jar and stomped off in disgust. The crowd scattered, and Laban sat down near the well.

"So, it worked, didn't it?" Laban slapped his sides and let go of a loud laugh. "There's nothing more satisfying than putting trouble to flight!"

"Honestly, Uncle, you really can be so difficult!"

"Thank you, Abby, my dear. Now shouldn't you be running along to the barley fields?"

"Yes, I'm on my way." She turned to leave.

"Abby. . ." Laban called his niece to his side. "Ruth works with you, doesn't she?"

"Yes."

Laban lowered his voice. "She's all right, isn't she? None of the men have bothered her, have they?"

Abigail smiled and took her uncle by the hand.

"She's fine. Boaz sees to that! He's warned all the men not to bother her."

Laban signed with relief. "She's so young and alone. I worry that someone might try. . ."

"Don't worry, Uncle," Abigail said. "Someone's looking out for her." She looked at Laban with questioning eyes. "If I didn't know better, Laban the independent, tough man, I'd say you care about that young Moabitess."

"Like she was my own daughter," he said quietly.

"You mean Laban the loner has feelings?" Abby grinned.

Laban touched his finger to his lips. "Don't tell anyone! It might ruin my image."

Abigail laughed. "Your secret's safe with me!" Laban watched as she hurried down the road toward the fields. The sun was already bright overhead, and it promised to be a sweltering day.

Ruth hummed a song of the harvest as she walked the familiar path to the fields. She paused when she came to a tall pomegranate tree. Among the dark green leaves flashed brilliant red blossoms. Ruth's eyes soaked in the bright colors. Suddenly, a rustle in the nearby bushes caught Ruth's attention. She stiffened with fear. She was too far from the village to run back and too far from the fields to call for help. Memories of the cruel shepherd on the plains of Moab flashed across her mind and paralyzed her with fear.

All at once, someone jumped out at Ruth from behind the bushes and almost knocked her down. Ruth screamed with fright.

It was a little boy.

Ruth caught her balance, and when she realized how small her attacker was, she laughed with relief.

The child had tumbled to the ground and was trying to get up and run.

"Hey!" Ruth reached for his chubby little hand and helped him to his feet.

The little boy's dark hair was a tangle of curls. He pushed the curls out of his eyes and looked up at Ruth.

"My grandma says that all Moabite women 'tice men of Israel to their doom. Are you going to 'tice me to my doom?" He made himself as tall as possible. "I'm a man, you know." His little chin quivered.

Ruth stifled a laugh. "I think the word is entice, and no, I am not going to entice you to your doom. You don't have to be afraid of me. You look like a very brave boy. What's your name?"

"Gideon."

"Where are you going in such a hurry?"

"Laban the merchant promised me a ride on one of his donkeys. He'll prob'ly put me on the meanest one 'cause I'm so brave."

Ruth nodded in agreement. "You better run along then, Brave Gideon."

Gideon grinned with satisfaction and hurried off to high adventure.

Ruth gazed with longing at the little figure running toward Bethlehem. In ten years of marriage to Mahlon, she had never been blessed with a baby. Her heart ached for a moment, but the bright sun reminded her there was work to do.

Every day Boaz came to the fields to check on the workers, and every day he greeted Ruth with a smile. His kindness made her feel at home in Bethlehem.

After a vigorous day's work, Ruth enjoyed climbing the outside stairs to the roof of their home. After enduring the heat of the fields, Ruth reveled in the cool caress of the evening breezes. One evening, Naomi joined her daughter-in-law on the roof. Ruth noticed that Naomi had an "I have a plan" look on her face.

"What's on your mind, Mother?" Ruth asked.

Naomi cleared her throat and looked lovingly at her daughter-in-law.

"Ruth, you have been so good to me. You have treated me as if I were your own mother. Now I want to do something for you." Ruth protested, but Naomi continued.

"After all you have done for me, shouldn't I try to find a home for you, a home where you would be well taken care of?" Naomi leaned forward earnestly. "In Israel, there is a special provision for the widow. If your husband dies and leaves no son to inherit his property, then a brother or close relative must marry the widow. The first son would be considered the dead husband's son, so his name and property would not be lost in Israel. And isn't Boaz our relative? That makes him a kinsman-redeemer."

"Boaz?" Thoughts of Boaz's strength and kindness filled Ruth's mind.

"Listen carefully, my dear. The barley harvest is almost over. Tonight Boaz will be winnowing barley at the threshing floor. Wash yourself, put on your perfume and your best clothes.

"Go down to the threshing floor and wait until Boaz is finished with the harvest meal. Don't let him see you. Then watch to see where he goes to sleep. Then go to him, uncover his feet, and lie down there. When he awakes, he will tell you what to do."

Ruth looked at her mother-in-law in amazement. Naomi's eyes were filled with love. "Trust me, Daughter."

"I will do whatever you want me to do," Ruth replied.

Naomi reached over and hugged Ruth tightly. "Hurry now, and get ready."

Inside the house, Ruth retrieved her long white tunic and her blue shawl from one of the baskets stacked in the corner of the room. She was ready in no time and with a final hug from her mother-in-law, Ruth left for the threshing floor. Naomi watched until Ruth disappeared down the road, her soft blue and white clothes blending with the tender blue haze of evening.

CHAPTER 11

At the threshing floor, Boaz and his men winnowed the barley. With large wooden forks, they flung the beaten grain into the air. The evening breezes carried away the light straw and dust, while the heavier kernels of barley fell to the floor. While they worked, their talk and laughter filled the air. It was a bountiful harvest, and the wheat fields promised to be bountiful as well.

Ruth drew near to the threshing floor and hid herself in the shadows of a myrtle tree.

"Boaz," a young boy called shyly to the man. "Tell us about the time some nomads attacked in the wheat fields and you ran them off all the way to the wilderness."

Boaz laughed and with strong arms pitched the grain into the air. "You've heard that story a thousand times!"

"Please," several young voices chimed in. "Tell us again!"

"All right, all right," said Boaz. "I can see I have no choice!"

Light from the torches lit up the large round threshing floor and the edges of the nearby fields. The eager faces of the youths shone in the flickering light, their eyes sparkling with expectation. Boaz noticed a little child among the group.

"Why, Gideon! What are you doing out here tonight?"

"My mother said I could watch the winning if Micah watched me!" He looked up at his older brother with a pleading look.

"It's winnowing, *not* winning, and if you don't keep quiet, I'll take you home right now!" Micah said impatiently.

"Okay, boys, let's not fight." Boaz smiled down at Gideon. "This story may be scary for you, young fellow."

"I'm Brave Gideon," the little soldier said proudly.

"Yeah, right," Micah whispered sarcastically. Gideon stuck out his tongue and turned his attention to Boaz.

"Several years ago, just before the wheat harvest, the Philistines had been raiding the fields of the neighboring villages. We knew it was only a matter of time before they came to Bethlehem."

The young boys' eyes grew wide. Gideon hid behind his brother.

"As you know, our village is small, and we didn't have enough men to fight them off, man for man; so we devised a plan."

"A plan?" Gideon whispered from behind Micah.

"Hush up." Micah frowned at his little brother.

"The raids were always carried out at night, when everyone was asleep. So Seth and I and a handful of men would keep watch every night. One night, our guard duty paid off. We discovered a band of the thieves in the middle of one of my fields." Boaz paused and looked up at the moon. "There was no moon that night, so it was hard to see."

"You mean it was dark?" Gideon asked.

"It was VERY dark," Seth said in a serious tone. The foreman hefted a shovelful of grain into the air. "Tell them what happened next, Boaz."

Boaz nodded and gave Gideon a wink.

"The Philistines had stationed their watchman at the edge of the field. Fortunately for us, he had fallen asleep. We stole his weapons and in the cover of the night, with only the stars shining above, we quickly lit the torches we had set up all around the field. We caught the thieves by surprise."

Seth continued. "Boaz yelled out, 'We've got you surrounded. If you don't get out, we'll set this field on fire and burn you alive!' The only thing those marauders could see were the torches. Well, they ran out of there as fast as they could, and Boaz chased them with their own spears toward the wilderness. And for all we know, they're still running!"

Boaz laughed and raked the grain into a pile. "We're almost finished here. Why don't you boys get something to eat?"

Boaz and the men finished the winnowing and joined the others and sat down at the harvest feast. The joy of a bountiful harvest shone on the faces of the people and their laughter danced in the night air. The torches joined the dance, gleaming and flickering in the breeze.

Ruth waited patiently in the shadows. Finally, the feast was over and most of the people returned to their homes. Boaz and a few workers remained at the threshing floor to guard the grain.

"It's been a good day's work," Boaz said to his men. "May the Lord bless you."

"The Lord bless you!" they answered.

Boaz lay down by the pile of grain and covered himself

with his cloak. His heart was warm with the happiness of the day, and he took a deep breath of the evening air.

Boaz sat up for a moment. There was a trace of perfume in the air.

That's funny, Boaz thought. *That smells like some kind of perfume.* He shook his head and laughed to himself. *I must be extra tired!*

Ruth waited until everyone was asleep. Then she softly walked over to Boaz. She was afraid the pounding of her heart would waken him. Carefully, she uncovered Boaz's feet and lay down. The flames of the torches had dwindled and Ruth looked up at the midnight sky. The stars greeted her with their customary sparkle and Ruth smiled, remembering her long journey from Moab.

"And look where the journey has brought me," she whispered to herself. "Oh, Lord, please be with me now." She began to tremble. What if Boaz didn't want her? After all, she was a foreigner! "No," she said to herself. "I won't be afraid. The living God will watch out for me."

In the deepest chamber of the night, the bark of a fox echoed in the hills and Boaz woke with a start. The gentle scent of perfume hung in the air like a fragrant messenger. Boaz turned over, and to his surprise there was someone lying at his feet.

"Who are you?" he whispered.

Ruth sat up.

"I am Ruth, your maidservant. Spread your cloak of protection over me, for you are a kinsman-redeemer."

Joy swept through Boaz's heart like a rushing wind.

"May the Lord give you happiness, young lady, because this loving-kindness you show tonight is even greater than the love you showed before in coming to Bethlehem. Instead of going after any of the younger men, rich or poor, you have chosen to come to me."

Ruth shivered in the moonlight.

"Now, don't be afraid, young lady. I will do all that you need for me to do. Surely all of Bethlehem knows what a woman of strength you are!"

Boaz continued in a whisper, while the other men dreamed of Philistine raids and harvest feasts.

"It's true that I am a near kinsman, but there is a man who is a closer relative than I am. Stay here tonight, and in the morning, if he will accept the role of kinsman-redeemer, very well, let him do so. But if he does not, I promise, as surely as the Lord lives, I will be your kinsman-redeemer. Stay here until the morning comes."

Ruth lay back at Boaz's feet. He gently covered her with his cloak. She wondered who the other relative was and what he was like. What if that man decided to redeem her? But Boaz was so strong and kind, surely the other man wouldn't— "Stop it," Ruth said to herself. She pulled her thoughts back to the truth that was now written on her heart—the living Lord would watch over her.

Boaz lay quietly looking at the moon while his heart pounded with joy. "I can't believe she came to me!" he said to himself. "She came to me! She's so beautiful and kind!

What if that man agrees to redeem Ruth?" He looked up at the night sky, mindful of the woman at his feet. *The Lord's hand is in this,* he thought to himself. *The Lord has a plan. He will lead the way.*

His thoughts became peaceful and the hours passed quickly. Early in the morning before the sun rose, Ruth got up quietly to leave. Boaz nodded his approval.

"It's good that you go now, while it is still dark." He looked at his sleeping workers. "We don't need ugly rumors flying through Bethlehem.

"Now bring your shawl over here and hold it out for me."

Ruth took off her shawl, and as she held it, Boaz filled it with six measures of barley.

Boaz placed the grain-filled shawl over Ruth's shoulders and smiled down at her. "I don't want you to turn to your mother-in-law with empty hands."

"Thank you," she whispered.

Ruth left the threshing floor and returned home. Naomi fluttered around her, with questions flying. "So what happened, Daughter? How did it go?"

She helped Ruth with her shawl and together they put the grain in one of the baskets. Ruth told Naomi everything that had happened. She held up the basket of grain.

"He sent this to you," she said with a smile.

Joyfully, Naomi clasped her hands together and motioned for Ruth to sit down.

"Stay here until you know how everything turns out." Naomi put on her own shawl and went to the door. "Boaz will not rest until he settles the matter today."

Naomi left the house and headed for the place where all legal business took place: the gate of the village.

CHAPTER 12

The gate of the village was already open and bustling with activity. Women were gathered at the well to draw water for the day; the nearby marketplace was open for business.

Boaz went to the gate and sat down to wait. He watched as people traveled in and out of the gate. They greeted him as they passed through, and Boaz smiled in return, barely noticing his friends and neighbors. But he kept watching the crowds carefully.

Hannah greeted Abigail at the well and put down her clay jug.

"Well, it's a busy morning in Bethlehem," she said brightly.

"It certainly is," responded Abigail. "Look, there's Boaz, sitting at the gate. I wonder what he's doing?"

"So it is! Maybe he's going to bring something up before the elders. There have been a few more raids in the last couple of weeks," said Hannah thoughtfully. "Maybe it's about that."

"I'd say he's looking for someone," Judith piped up.

Hannah looked at Judith. "How can you tell?"

"Just look at him!" Judith said. "He's watching those crowds like an eagle searching for prey. I say he's looking for someone!"

"You're right," agreed Abigail. "I wonder who. . ."

"Hush now," interrupted Hannah. "Here comes Laban."

"Good morning, ladies." He smiled broadly. "How is everything at the well today? Is there still water in the well of Bethlehem? And who is it you are staring at?"

He followed their gaze to the gate.

"So it's Boaz you're concerned with today. Shall I go and tell him you're watching out for him? I'm sure it would put his mind at ease!"

"Oh, Uncle Laban." Abigail sighed.

"Why don't you mind your own business?" snorted Judith.

Laban laughed out loud and headed for the marketplace.

"I've got some fine pottery from Moab for sale, ladies," he called back to them. "And lamb's wool, too!"

Finally, Boaz spotted the man he was looking for. He called out to him. "Ethan! Come here and sit down at the gate."

The man came over and sat down next to Boaz. "What is it, Boaz?"

"I have some business to conduct with you. Will you wait here while I gather together the ten elders of the village?"

"I will wait," he said.

Boaz left and called together the ten elders of Bethlehem and asked them to assemble at the gate. Soon a curious crowd gathered near the gate.

"What do you suppose—?" Hannah whispered to Abigail.

"Look! There's Naomi! What's she doing here?"

"Be quiet!" Judith hissed. "I can't hear a thing."

Boaz sat down next to the man named Ethan. All eyes were on Boaz as he began to speak. The morning sun glittered above the scene, and all was quiet except for the occasional braying of a donkey and the cry of a baby lamb.

"Thank you all for being here," Boaz began. He nodded to the elders and turned toward Ethan.

"As you know, Naomi has returned from Moab under difficult circumstances. Because of this, she is going to sell the property that belonged to her husband Elimelech."

"Just as I thought!" whispered Judith.

"Shh!" Hannah leaned forward to get a better look.

"I wanted to let you know about this, so that you can buy it, with these people and the elders as witnesses. If you want to buy it, then do so. You are the next of kin to Elimelech, the land is rightfully yours. However, if you do not want to redeem this property, let me know now. After you, I am the closest relative."

Naomi's heart pounded as she waited to hear the man's reply. The crowd strained with excitement. Laban watched with concern in his eyes.

The man's eyes lit up at the thought of adding more property to his own. He stroked his beard and stood to his feet.

"I will redeem it."

The crowd burst into a torrent of chatter. Laban spat into the dust, but Naomi kept her eyes on Boaz.

"Very well," replied Boaz firmly. He stood to his feet beside Ethan. His tall, strong frame towered over his relative. "But when you redeem the property of Naomi and Ruth the Moabitess, you must marry the wife of the deceased and give her a son. It is the duty of a kinsman to keep the name of the dead alive along with his inheritance."

Ethan's face darkened with worry. "Ruth the Moabitess! If I marry her, that would ruin my own inheritance! I can't do that. You redeem it yourself. I just can't." Ethan pulled off his sandal and held it out to Boaz.

In those days in Israel, a business deal was made legal by the seller giving the buyer his sandal. Ethan was offering Boaz the right to redeem Naomi and Ruth's property.

Boaz bowed graciously and took the sandal. He turned to face the elders seated at the gate and the crowd assembled there and held the sandal up in the air.

"On this day, you are witnesses that I have purchased all the property of Elimelech, and all that belonged to Chilion and Mahlon." His voice filled the air. "You are also witnesses that I have chosen Ruth the Moabitess to be my wife, in order to keep the name of Mahlon alive along with his inheritance. His name will not be cut off from among his family, nor from the place of his nativity."

The crowd boiled over with joy. The elders stood and nodded their approval. "We are witnesses," they said. Everyone began shouting all at once. "We are witnesses!"

One of the elders lifted his hands to heaven. "May the Lord cause the woman coming into your house to be like Rachel and Leah, who built the house of our father Israel. May you be great and prosper in the land of Ephrathah, and may you be famous in Bethlehem.

"May the Lord make your house like the house of Perez, the son of Tamar and the royal line of Judah, because of the children the Lord will give you through this young woman."

"Amen!" everyone shouted.

Naomi wept for joy, and the women surrounded her with cries of happiness. There was a steady flow of congratulations, and plans were quickly made for a feast to celebrate the new marriage. In the midst of all the happy commotion, Boaz slipped away from the crowd.

CHAPTER 13

Ruth sat alone in the little house, wondering what was happening down at the village gate. The faithful oil lamp sputtered and glowed, and Ruth watched the flame cast its light against the wall.

She marveled at the events of the last few days, and her heart beat faster when she thought of the night before. What would happen today? Who would come and get her? Who would be her kinsman-redeemer?

"Ruth!" Startled at the sound of a voice at the door, the young woman turned around to see Boaz standing in the doorway. It was the first time he had ever called her by name.

The man's voice danced in the air and struck a chord of remembrance in Ruth's heart. It was as if she had heard his voice a long time ago, before she ever knew him. Ruth closed her eyes and listened.

As Boaz called out her name again, suddenly Ruth understood. The Lord, the living God, knew her name! He loved her and would always take care of her. She had come to trust under the Lord's wings, Boaz had said. Now she knew God had given her Boaz! But beyond the tender care of those she could see and touch, Ruth saw the living God. She knew she would never be alone again, no matter what the future held for her.

Ruth was speechless. Boaz walked over and gently took

her by the hand.

"It's all right," he said softly. "You are my wife now."

The young widow looked up and saw the love in Boaz's heart shining through his eyes. She let the joy of the moment wash over her in waves of comfort.

"Thank you," she finally spoke, softly.

Boaz put his arms around Ruth. "And don't worry about Naomi. She'll live with us." He smiled down at her. "Let's go home."

The sound of laughter and excited voices filled the air as Naomi and her friends approached her house. Boaz and Ruth greeted them at the door and Naomi enveloped Ruth in a warm hug.

"I am so happy for you!" Naomi cried. "The Lord has not forgotten us!" She looked up at Boaz with deep respect in her eyes. "And thanks to you, the names of my husband and my sons will not be lost in Israel." Naomi bowed to the ground before Ruth's kinsman-redeemer.

Boaz shook his head and helped Naomi to her feet.

"It is my privilege," he said. "Not another word about it. Now let's go! I imagine the celebration has already begun!"

"You run along," Naomi urged the couple. "I have something I have to do first."

Boaz and Ruth left Naomi in the house and her friends joined them. Naomi looked around the small house that had been her home. Memories of Mahlon and Chilion chasing each other around the room crowded her thoughts and she smiled. She could hear Elimelech scolding them and laughing at their antics.

Naomi gathered the happy memories from every corner of the room, but decided to leave the sorrow behind. She found the basket she was looking for and changed her clothes.

When she arrived at the celebration, Ruth noticed the change immediately.

"Mother!" she exclaimed. "Your sackcloth!"

"It's gone," replied Naomi.

"You look wonderful!"

Boaz's home was overflowing with guests. Boaz's servants busily prepared the food and wine for the midday feast. It seemed like all of Bethlehem was coming to take part in the celebration.

Ruth was overwhelmed with all the attention, so she retreated to the roof of Boaz's home. She looked down at the courtyard below and watched as more people joined the party. The sun was brilliant and hot, but Ruth preferred to stay on the roof. The wheat fields surrounding Bethlehem swayed like golden ripples in the breeze, and the terraced hills boasted an abundance of olive and grape vineyards. Beyond the vineyards and fields of grain, flocks of sheep and goats speckled the land with black and white.

"It's a beautiful place, isn't it?" A familiar voice spoke.

Ruth twirled around. "Laban!"

"I am so proud of you," the merchant said with a smile.

Ruth laughed. "Thank you! I'm glad you're here, Laban. I wanted to thank you again for all your help and especially for saving my life. How could I ever repay you?"

"Forget it," Laban said.

"Oh, I'll never forget it. And I told Boaz all about it."

"You didn't have to do that," Laban protested.

Ruth stubbornly shook her head. "We'll never forget it."

Laban laughed. "I know when I'm beaten!"

The two stood together silently for a few moments, surveying the lovely landscape. The hills of Judea rolled faithfully to the horizon in shades of green and blue. Laban turned his eyes eastward and then looked at Ruth.

"I know a way you can repay me," he said.

"Wonderful!" Ruth replied. "What can I do for you?"

"Listen to me tell you one more story."

Ruth clapped her hands together. "Of course! I'd love to hear another story." She sat down and motioned for Laban to do the same. The merchant bowed to the young lady and took a seat beside her.

Laban pointed toward the east. "Beyond the wilderness of Judea, as you know, lies the Jordan River Valley. You remember what I told you about Moses?"

Ruth nodded eagerly. "He led the people out of Egypt and climbed the mountain to speak with the Lord."

"Yes, yes, that's right!" said Laban. "And it was on the Plains of Moab that the people camped before entering the Promised Land."

The poplar trees and the smell of the Salt Sea paraded before Ruth's mind.

"They crossed over to Jericho, right?"

"Yes, that's right. Now Moses died, and a brave man

named Joshua became the leader. He planned to conquer Jericho, but first he sent spies to the city. Those two spies went to the house of a Canaanite prostitute named Rahab to get information."

"Did she help them?" Ruth interrupted.

"She certainly did!" Laban replied.

"When the king of Jericho heard there were spies in the city, he sent a search party to look for them. Rahab hid them on the roof of her home."

"Why did she do that? Then what happened?"

"Will you let me tell the story?" Laban rolled his eyes in exasperation.

"I won't say another word."

"All right then. Now, where was I? Oh yes, Rahab hid the spies on the roof of her home. After the king's men left, Rahab went up to the roof and told the men she had heard how their God had delivered the Israelites out of Egypt and defeated all their enemies on the way. She told them she knew their God was the God of heaven and earth, and she asked that she and her family be spared when the Israelites attacked Jericho."

"Did they. . ." Laban scowled and Ruth covered her mouth with her hand.

"The spies agreed to show her mercy and instructed her to tie a scarlet cord in the window of her home. They told her to have all her family in her house and to stay in the house until the fighting was over. No one would attack the house with the scarlet cord.

"The Lord told Joshua to have the people march around Jericho six days. On the seventh day they blew on their trumpets and let out a shout. The walls of Jericho fell to the ground in a roar of rubble."

Ruth's eyes were wide with wonder, but she didn't say a word.

"The Lord gave them the victory, and Jericho was completely destroyed." Laban paused. "Everything, except for Rahab's family."

The listener with the auburn hair sighed with relief.

"Rahab lived with the Israelites for the rest of her life. An Israelite named Salmon married her, and they had a son. In fact, she just died a few years ago."

"A few years ago!" Ruth blurted out. "Did you know her, Laban?"

Laban nodded. "The name of her son is Boaz."

The impact of Laban's words resounded in Ruth's heart. She was stunned.

"You mean Boaz's mother was. . .a Canaanite?"

"Yes, she was. Rahab embraced the faith of the Israelites when she heard of the power of their God. Her life was spared because of the kindness she showed to the spies when she hid them from the king."

Ruth's eyes filled with tears. "What a merciful, wonderful God! It had to be the Lord who led me to the fields of Boaz, to a man who would look beyond my nationality and see my heart. Oh, Laban," Ruth wept, "thank you so much for telling me!"

Laban turned away so Ruth would not see his tears. "It's all right," he mumbled.

Laban stood to his feet. "I have to go now. I'm leaving early tomorrow for Joppa. I've got some business there to take care of."

Ruth wiped her tears and gave Laban a hug. "Thank you for everything."

They heard the sound of hurried steps on the stairway. It was Boaz.

"There you are!" he said warmly. "I've been looking all over for you. It's time for the feast and everyone is waiting for the bride!"

Ruth blushed at the word bride. "I'm so happy I can hardly breathe!"

"Ruth!" Naomi's voice called up from the courtyard.

"Coming!" she called back. "Good-bye, Laban. I hope we see you again soon." With that, the young woman hurried down the stairs to her mother-in-law.

Boaz placed his hand on Laban's shoulder. "I want to thank you for all you've done for Ruth. She told me how you saved her life. I will always be grateful to you. If you ever need my help, just let me know."

"Thank you, Boaz, but you know me! I don't need any-one's help!" He laughed and slapped his friend on the back. "Congratulations on your new wife." He lowered his voice. "Take good care of her, Boaz. She's like a daughter to me."

"You know I will! Now, come join the feast!"

The feast lasted the whole day and well into the night. The

next day, it was a happy memory, and one year later another celebration was held. Ruth gave birth to a baby boy.

The women of the neighborhood named him Obed, which means "servant."

"Praise be to the Lord," Hannah exclaimed to Naomi. "The Lord has given you a kinsman-redeemer! May this child be famous in Israel! He will restore your life and care for you when you are old." She looked at Ruth. "For your daughter-in-law, who loves you dearly and is better to you than seven sons, has given birth to him."

Naomi took the baby and held it in her arms. "I never thought I'd have a grandson! Blessed be the Lord!"

Boaz's home resounded with the happy sounds of celebration in honor of Ruth's firstborn son.

The autumn rain was falling steadily now and the reds and yellows of the poppies blurred together in the downpour.

A strong voice called to the young woman.

"Ruth! You're getting drenched." Boaz wrapped his cloak around her and they walked back to the house together. The rain showered the land with refreshment and mingled with Ruth's gentle tears of joy.

She was home.

When Obed, the son of Boaz and Ruth, grew up, he had a son named Jesse. When Jesse grew up, he had a boy who one day killed a giant by the name of Goliath. He killed him with a stone from his slingshot. That boy later became king of Israel. His name was David.

Many generations later another boy was born in Bethlehem, descended from David, descended from Obed. His name was Jesus.

ESTHER

COURAGEOUS QUEEN

by Susan Martins Miller

CHAPTER 1

The lively children giggled and chased each other down the road, while the women talked quietly among themselves. Occasionally a mother would raise her voice slightly or give a stern look to a child who was wandering too far away or getting too loud. This was an ordinary part of the day—drawing water from the well late in the afternoon and walking back to the row of modest houses where the Jews lived in the city of Susa.

Esther walked with the women now, although most of them were older than she was. She did not often have much to contribute to their conversation, which was usually about husbands and children. She did not truly fit in, but somehow she did not fit in with the energetic, squealing children either. She had grown past that stage. She was not a child, but she was not quite a woman.

As the group turned the last corner of the dusty road leading home, Esther's heart began to pound, and she could hear the gasps of the women around her. Soldiers were leaving their street! This could only mean one thing. Once again they had come to take a beautiful young woman to become part of the king's harem. Esther ran as fast as she could. Water sloshed out of the heavy jug in her arms. When she reached her own house, she threw open the wooden door and began to shout.

"Uncle! Uncle!" Esther hurried from room to room looking for her uncle Mordecai, who had taken her in when she was orphaned and raised her as his own daughter. "Uncle Mordecai, where are you?"

She found him sitting silently in his own room. "Esther, Darling," he said, "come sit with me."

Esther stood still and demanded the truth.

"They've taken someone again, haven't they?" Esther's voice shook with fear. "Tell me who, Uncle. Who was it?"

Mordecai was very slow to answer. At last he said in a hushed whisper, "Rebekah."

Esther put her hand to her mouth to stop the scream that welled up inside her. "Rebekah? My friend, Rebekah? But Uncle, Rebekah is no older than I am."

Mordecai reached out and pulled Esther down on the bench beside him. She laid her head on his shoulder as he stroked her hair.

"Esther, you are very beautiful."

"Oh, Uncle, you have been telling me that all my life. You just say that because you love me."

"No, Esther. This time I say it as a warning. It has been almost a year now since King Xerxes began his search for a new queen. And you have changed so much during this year. You no longer look like a child. You are becoming a woman, and you are very beautiful."

Esther sat up straight and looked at her uncle's worried face. "You think they will come for me, don't you, Uncle?"

"Yes, Esther, I do."

The girl stood up and stomped her foot. "But, Uncle, how many women does the king need to choose from? The soldiers have already rounded up hundreds from among the Persians and Jews. Surely one of them has pleased the king."

Mordecai shook his head sadly. "I cannot explain it, Esther. And I pray that it will not happen to you." He paused and brightened his face. "Come, my child, let us have our meal."

Reluctantly, Esther took the hand her uncle offered, and they went together to the small room where they prepared their food together each evening. Mordecai tried several times to begin a conversation about a more pleasant subject, but Esther did not respond. She felt such an odd mixture of feelings: anger at the king's cruel method of choosing a new queen; grief for her friend Rebekah; fear that she, too, would be taken from her home and forced into a strange life. For years she had been yearning to grow up and take her place in the adult world; now she wished she could remain a child—at least until the king chose his new queen.

Esther went about her daily tasks as usual for the next several days. She cleaned the house, kept the water jug full, and made sure her uncle had good food to eat each evening. She loved to go to the marketplace and choose the vegetables and argue with the merchants about a fair price. Some of them pretended to hide when they saw her coming with her basket slung over her arm. This was a game they had been playing with Esther since she was a small girl and had come with her uncle to the market each day. Now she came alone, and the playful bartering still made it fun.

"Joseph, I want only the best vegetables you have today," she said, as she said every day.

"Then you will have to pay the best price," he answered. Esther's favorite merchant placed a tray of fresh vegetables in front of her and watched as she began her selection.

"This one is too soft; I will not pay full price," she said authoritatively. "And this one is too small; you picked it too soon."

"Very well. I will sell those to someone who is not such an expert as you are." Joseph smiled at Esther. Then something behind him caught his eyes and his smile faded quickly. He spoke urgently. "Esther, you must hide! Right now!"

It was too late. Before Esther could respond to Joseph's warning, her elbow was grabbed roughly and she was spun around to look straight into the eyes of a soldier. Her basket was knocked to the ground. Quickly she looked around. There were several other soldiers nearby, their swords ready. No one could risk helping her.

"Uncle!" she screamed. "Find my uncle!" Joseph had already run off toward the business district where Mordecai worked, close to the king's palace. As she was dragged along, Esther looked frantically through the crowd, searching for her uncle's full dark beard and distinctive, wide-set eyes. She was afraid she would be taken to the palace and never allowed to see her uncle again.

Suddenly Mordecai burst through the crowd and blocked the way of the soldiers. "Let her go," he demanded. "She's only a child." Esther clutched for her uncle's arm and held on tightly.

"Perhaps she is a child in your eyes," the soldier responded. "But she will be prepared to meet the king as a woman. Her beauty is obvious even now, and with the right adornment, she will be very lovely." He began to push her forward again. Esther tightened her grip on Mordecai's arm, and he moved quickly to keep up with the long strides of the soldier. Familiar faces flew past them—neighbors, friends, merchants—would she ever see these people again? Rebekah's mother was in the crowd, her face twisted in anguish. For a fleeting moment, Esther was comforted by the thought that she might see Rebekah again.

Abruptly another soldier raised his arm to stop Mordecai's movement. When he resisted, her uncle was struck and knocked to the ground, stunned. The distance between them grew rapidly, and she knew he would never catch up.

"Uncle! Uncle!"

There was no answer.

"Oh, Rebekah, your skin has such a lovely color," Esther said to her friend. "That new cream Hegai gave you is really working."

"Thank you, Esther," her friend answered. "Hegai is pleased with the results." She shrugged her shoulders. "But I don't really care. Why does it matter what my skin looks like?"

Esther sighed in agreement. "I know. We've been here for four years. We spend all our time making ourselves beautiful. The whole reason is to please the king and be chosen as his queen—and we don't want to be queen."

"All I want is to go home," Rebekah groaned. "They give us special food, expensive perfumes, beauty treatments, oil baths, maids to wait on us. And it's all for nothing. We'll never have husbands to appreciate our beauty. We'll always be part of the king's harem, and he doesn't even know our names."

The conversation was interrupted by a gentle knock on Esther's door.

"Come in," she called.

One of her seven maids stepped into the room. "Your uncle is outside the palace, Esther."

"In the usual place?" Esther asked, moving toward the large window at the end of her room.

"Yes, Ma'am."

Esther carefully drew back the edge of the curtain and looked out. For many years, Mordecai had held an important job that allowed him to be near the palace. Hegai, the servant in charge of the young women waiting to be called by the king, had taken a special liking to Esther as soon as she had entered the palace. He had given her comfortable rooms in the best part of the palace and freedom to move about the courtyards if she wished. If she was careful, she could talk to Mordecai quite often.

Casually, Esther wrapped a light shawl around her slender shoulders and strolled down the hallway and out into the courtyard, bright with sunlight. Hegai would be alarmed if she exposed her flawless skin to direct sunlight, but he had agreed that fresh air would add color to her cheeks. She had long ago convinced him to allow her to take vigorous walks around the courtyard, as long as she stayed out of the sun.

Esther walked once around the courtyard and then selected a low stone bench set close to the high palace wall and under a generous shade tree. She began to whistle a familiar melody from her girlhood. Soon she heard her uncle's voice.

"How are you, my dear niece?" Mordecai's soft voice came clearly through a spot where the stones in the wall were not quite joined.

Esther smiled briefly and answered, "I am fine, Uncle. I am so glad you came today. I only wish I could see your face instead of talking to you through this wall."

"And how is Rebekah? Her mother sends her love."

"She is very homesick, Uncle. She wants to go home. We all do. But tell her mother that Rebekah looks lovely and rested."

"You have not told them, have you, Esther?"

"That I am Jewish?" she answered. Mordecai asked this question every time they spoke together. "No, Uncle, I have not. But I still do not understand why it must be a secret. Surely they knew they were taking Jewish girls when they rounded us up."

"I cannot explain, Esther. I just have a feeling that things would not go well for you if they knew you were Jewish right now."

"Perhaps they would let me come home. Perhaps the king does not want a Jewish queen."

Mordecai did not answer right away. "Let's not argue. We don't have time for that."

Esther hid her frustration. "Yes, Uncle."

"I must go now. I will come again."

Esther sat on the bench for several minutes, looking around and wondering if anyone had seen her talking. Since Mordecai was out of sight, it would seem as if she were talking to herself, and that would surely lead to questions. Satisfied that she had not been seen, Esther got up and walked around the courtyard one more time.

When she returned to her room, Hegai was waiting for her.

"I've been looking all over for you, Esther," he said sternly.

Esther's heart was pounding. Perhaps someone had seen her after all. "I was in the courtyard, taking a walk. You have given your approval for that."

Hegai shook his head and waved his hand. "No, it's not that, Esther. I came to tell you it's your turn."

"My turn?" she questioned.

"Yes. Your turn to go to the king."

Now her heart felt as if it would stop beating. She had not thought this would ever really happen. "When?" she asked.

"In three days," Hegai answered. "You may choose anything in the harem to take with you—your clothes, your perfumes, a gift for the king. Choose carefully, Esther. You are so very beautiful. Perhaps you will be the one to please the king."

Hegai left, and Esther stood motionless for a long time. After four years in the king's harem, even Esther had come to believe that she truly was a beautiful young woman. But was she beautiful enough to be chosen as queen? If she were chosen, would she be able to see Mordecai openly and often?

The door swung open, and Rebekah ran in breathlessly.

"I just heard! Oh, Esther, what are you going to do?"

"I. . .I. . .I'm not sure. I suppose I should ask Hegai's advice. He has been so kind to me."

The next three days were a flurry of activity for Esther and Hegai. Rebekah was always nearby, wanting to spend every moment possible with her friend. Esther trusted Hegai's advice and made her choices simply. The clothes she selected flattered her delicate frame and distinctive coloring. She would not pretend to be someone she was not; she was a simple girl with natural beauty, and this is what she presented to the king. When she was introduced to King Xerxes, she bowed deeply and followed meekly as she was led to his rooms.

The next morning, the palace buzzed with the news that

King Xerxes was going to make a proclamation. Esther stood in the courtyard and gazed up at the balcony where the king would appear. The royal trumpeters stepped forward, raised their instruments, and announced the arrival of King Xerxes.

In a loud voice for all to hear, Xerxes said simply, "I have found my queen. There shall be a great royal banquet in honor of Queen Esther."

CHAPTER 3

Mordecai sat very still and held his breath, hardly able to believe that what he was hearing could be true. He had his back pressed to the wall outside the palace, afraid even to breathe. The conversation just around the corner reached his ears easily during a moment when not many people were nearby.

"Tonight at midnight," the hushed voice said. "We will enter the palace at the end of our shift and wait for the moment to come."

Another voice answered in a harsh whisper. "The knife will be under my cloak. When dawn comes, the people will awake and be glad that we have gotten rid of King Xerxes."

The voices trailed away, covered by the shuffling of feet. Cautiously, Mordecai let out his breath and stepped silently to the corner. Slowly he looked around the edge of the wall at the backs of the two men walking away as their cloaks fluttered in the breeze. Even though they had whispered, Mordecai thought he had recognized the voices, and now he was sure who the men were. They had never caused trouble before; they simply stood guard at the palace gate day after day, making conversation with those who passed by. Even Mordecai had spoken to them quite frequently. And now these two soldiers were conspiring to kill the king. They stood guard under the authority of Haman, one of the king's highest officials. Mordecai had never liked Haman, even when they were young boys, but he could hardly believe that Haman would be involved in such an evil plot.

Mordecai found a bench and sat down, trying to appear calm while he thought things through. What would Haman have to gain from trying to kill the king? Xerxes had already promoted him to a very high level. Perhaps Haman had nothing to do with it; perhaps the men were planning to overthrow Haman as well. If Xerxes were killed, what would happen to Esther? The longer Mordecai sat, the more confusing questions flooded his mind and made it hard for him to think clearly.

Stroking his beard, Mordecai made up his mind. Esther had to be told. There was no way Xerxes would listen to someone like Mordecai, but Esther was the new queen, and she was the only one who could possibly get Xerxes to believe his life was threatened.

Mordecai hurried around to the palace gate. Ever since Esther had been made queen, they had been able to see each other in the outer courtyard where Esther received many of her visitors. Although they were surrounded by many other people, it was better than whispering through a crack in the wall. As usual, he was admitted to the courtyard and a servant was sent to inform Esther of his arrival.

As soon as she saw Mordecai, the beautiful queen knew something was terribly wrong.

"Uncle! What is it?" She clutched his arm in alarm. "Are you ill?"

"No, Esther, nothing like that. But your husband is in danger."

"My husband?" Esther was puzzled. What would her uncle know about the king's business?

"I overheard some men talking today while I was working. I know who they are, Esther, and they mean business. It was Bigthana and Teresh, two of the officers who stand guard at the gate."

"What are you talking about, Uncle?"

"They want to kill the king! Tonight! At midnight. You must tell him, Esther, for your own sake. If something happens to Xerxes, do you really think they would have any use for you?"

The color drained from Esther's face as the truth of what Mordecai said sunk in. "All right," she said, "tell me what you heard."

Mordecai retold the whole conversation and explained what he knew about the officers he had seen and heard.

"I do not know if the king will believe me," Esther said at last. She knew Mordecai would not make up a plot like the one he described, but she was not sure the king would believe it. "But I will try to speak to him and tell him what you have said."

Mordecai paced back and forth outside the palace gate all day. When it was time for the midday meal, he hardly noticed. Instead, he kept walking. He forced himself to stroll casually and stop to talk to people every few minutes, trying not to appear concerned about anything unusual. Each time he passed Bigthana and Teresh standing at the gate, he nodded politely and acted as naturally as he could. As the hours wore on, he began to wonder if Esther would reach the king in time. It was now late in the afternoon. Soon it would be time for new guards to come to stand at the gate during the night. Bigthana and Teresh would be difficult to follow. Mordecai would not be allowed inside the palace, but the guards would surely find a way past their fellow soldiers. *Where is Esther?* he wondered. *What could possibly be keeping her so long?*

The end of the day came, and Bigthana and Teresh turned over their duties to other guards. Just as Mordecai had feared, they withdrew into the protection of the palace itself. Before they were out of sight, Mordecai saw Teresh softly touch his side, as if checking on the weapon he planned to use that night. Mordecai could only go as far as the courtyard to wait for word from Esther. In only minutes, Bigthana and Teresh were inside the palace and out of sight. Unable to sit still, Mordecai continued his pacing, circling the courtyard over and over, faster and faster.

Suddenly, Haman barged into the courtyard from inside the palace.

"Mordecai!" he shouted. "How dare you?"

"Did you know about this, Haman? Were these men acting on your orders?"

"I don't know what you are talking about," Haman said spitefully. Everyone could see his hatred for Mordecai. "Because of you, two of my finest officers are going to be hanged. According to the queen, it was you who accused the two guards of plotting to kill the king. How dare you get involved in matters that are none of your business."

Mordecai answered quietly, "The well-being of the king is the business of every citizen."

"Why must you use every opportunity to stir up trouble?" Haman was red in the face and speaking very loudly.

Mordecai remained calm. "I simply did my duty. If the officers are guilty, that is their own fault. I am not responsible for the punishment they face." He turned to walk away.

"You will pay for this!" Haman shouted. "I am more powerful than you realize!"

Mordecai stopped in his steps and started to respond to Haman. But he stopped himself before he spoke. The important thing was that Esther was safe. There would be no point in arguing further with Haman. Feeling the eyes of the crowd on him, Mordecai forced himself to take steady, straight steps until he was once again on the street outside the palace.

"Can you believe that the king has promoted Haman again?" said the old man, Joseph, to Mordecai one morning in the marketplace.

"Haman has been a very efficient officer," said Mordecai, trying to be kind. He had a lot of things on his mind, and he did not wish to stand in the street discussing Haman. He lifted his eyes to survey the vegetables.

"Mordecai, you know as well as I do that Haman is simply hungry for power," Joseph insisted. "He'll be telling King Xerxes what to do before long."

Mordecai nodded his head. Unfortunately, what Joseph said was probably true. Mordecai had never understood why Xerxes preferred Haman over all the other royal officials, but he had been promoted very rapidly. There was no denying that he had a strong influence on the king. Many people thought he even gave orders that the king did not know about.

Joseph continued talking. "I heard that the king has ordered all the royal officials to kneel and honor Haman when he passes by."

Mordecai stiffened up. "I will not do that. I will give the king the respect he deserves, but I cannot honor a man who hates my people."

"Then there's going to be trouble, Mordecai," Joseph warned. "It's common knowledge that Haman already has a grudge against you."

Mordecai kept his word. Day after day, he refused to kneel down or honor Haman. All the other officials obeyed the king's order that Haman be honored, and they watched Mordecai carefully to see if he would change his mind.

"Mordecai, you must kneel when Haman passes by," they said.

"I will not honor Haman," he answered.

"But it is the king's command," they countered. "When you do not honor Haman, you disobey the king."

When they questioned him, Mordecai would only repeat, "I will not honor Haman."

When word reached Haman that Mordecai would not kneel in his honor, he was enraged. "How dare he disobey the king's command!" Haman marched angrily through the halls of the palace scheming to punish Mordecai for his actions. His assistant almost had to run to keep up with him.

"It would be simple enough to ask the king to have Mordecai hanged from the gallows," one of his assistants suggested. "It would be an example, in case there are others who decide they do not wish to honor you."

"Yes, yes, a very good idea," answered Haman. "But Mordecai is a Jew. If he can cause this sort of trouble, will there not be others who will do the same? Perhaps we can find a way to get rid of all the Jews."

"A brilliant idea, Sir! The Jews could rise up and cause trouble for the king at any time. Mordecai may become their leader. It is best to be rid of them."

"I am sure I can get Xerxes to agree that the Jews are a threat and should be removed," Haman said confidently. "We must decide when and how. We shall cast the pur[1] and let the fates decide the date."

The date was set for eleven months away. "Good," said Haman with satisfaction. "That will give us plenty of time to persuade the king and make all the arrangements. We want to be sure we are thorough." They continued their discussions for several days until Haman had decided exactly what he would say to King Xerxes.

As soon as he had an opportunity, Haman spoke to Xerxes. "My good king," he said, "the king is a generous and powerful man. But we must be on the alert for threats to the king's power. There is a certain group of people scattered throughout the kingdom who may cause trouble. Their customs are different from ours, and they do not obey the king's commands. I believe that it would be in the king's best interest to destroy these people so that the kingdom may remain strong."

Haman paused to judge the king's response.

"Continue," said the king.

"If it pleases the king," Haman said, "let a decree be issued to destroy them. I will put a great sum of money into the royal treasury for the men who carry out this command."

Xerxes lifted his hand and removed the signet ring from his finger and gave it to Haman. "Haman, you are my highest

---

[1] Pur is the Hebrew word for "lot."

official. I know you are loyal and I trust your judgment. You may write up this decree and seal it with my ring so that it becomes law. But keep the money, and do with the people as you please."

Haman excitedly hurried back to his own rooms where his assistants were waiting for him. "That was even easier than I thought it would be," he said. He pulled out the royal signet ring and held it up for them to see. "We got just what we wanted, and it will not cost us anything. Now let's get organized!"

Immediately, Haman's assistants sent for the royal secretaries, and he began dictating the decree that would make it lawful for Persians to kill the Jews and steal their belongings. The secretaries worked day and night without relief. Haman was pressing to be sure the decree was drawn up before Xerxes could change his mind. He would often hold the royal ring in his hand and feel himself filled with the power it represented.

There were more than a hundred provinces in the kingdom and many different languages. Haman made sure that the governor of each province would receive the orders in the proper language. He called in translators to be sure that everything was exactly right. One day was chosen as the day when all the Jews could be killed. All the people of the kingdom were urged to be good citizens and obey the king's command. There was plenty of time for the decree to be delivered to the provinces and for the Persians to prepare to carry it out. Haman personally sealed each copy of the decree with the powerful royal ring of Xerxes, making it a law that could not be revoked.

Satisfied that all was in order, Haman called for the royal couriers. These young men would race to the far corners of the kingdom with copies of the new law. The proud official watched as his assistants handed out the copies and sent the couriers off on their journeys, urging them to go as quickly as possible.

Haman was already deciding how he would personally be sure that Mordecai was killed. Once again, he held up the royal ring and gloated as it sparkled in the light.

The crowd gathering in the street grew larger and larger as more and more people stopped to watch the old man tearing his clothes and wailing loudly and bitterly.

"What's he doing?" someone asked.

"He's a Jew," someone else answered. "It's a funny custom they have, I suppose."

Laughter rippled through the crowd as people joked about the strange man, who seemed unaware of the audience pressing in around him.

"I think it has something to do with the king's decree about the Jews," someone suggested. "I saw some other Jews behaving this way—but at least they stayed in their own homes instead of making a public spectacle in the middle of the street."

Joseph nudged his way through the crowd until he could see what was going on. He gasped when he realized who the man was. "Mordecai," he said aloud, without realizing it.

"Joseph, haven't you heard the king's command? How can you stay in the marketplace selling vegetables when Haman is plotting to destroy our people?" demanded Mordecai as he continued to rip his cloak and moan with grief.

Joseph reached out for Mordecai. "Please, my friend, why don't we find a place to sit down and talk about this." Joseph was whispering. He did not want to embarrass himself, but he could not abandon his old friend in the street.

Mordecai pushed Joseph off roughly. "Get away!" he shouted. "If you do not feel the horror of the crime that is being done to our people, then you are no friend of mine." Mordecai began to move up the street toward the city square in front of the king's gate. Some of the crowd lost interest and went on their way, but many people followed Mordecai, still amused by his odd behavior. Joseph moved along with the crowd, trying desperately to think of some way to make Mordecai stop before there was more trouble.

As they neared the palace, some of the guards and servants came out to watch. At last Joseph saw someone he recognized. "Please, hurry and tell the queen that her uncle is almost naked in the street," Joseph told the servant urgently. "Perhaps she can convince him to listen to reason."

When Esther heard the news, she acted quickly. She gathered some clothes together and gave them to a servant. "Hathach, take these clothes to Mordecai. Tell him that I have sent them so that he will not disgrace himself." Anxiously, she watched from a window to see what was happening in the street below. Mordecai was continuing to tear his clothes to shreds and cry out loudly with every rip as if he were in pain.

"I have no need to cover myself," shouted Mordecai when the clothes were given to him. "Tell Esther that she should join my mourning, rather than trying to make me stop."

Hathach the servant obediently reported Mordecai's words to the queen, who leaned further out the window to watch her uncle while trying to decide what to do.

"Hathach," she said, "please find out exactly what my uncle is mourning and why he is behaving this way. Ask him what he wants from me."

This time Hathach was gone a long time. Esther could see Mordecai gesturing and waving around a piece of parchment. Even the full beard covering his features did not hide the redness of anger in Mordecai's face. If only she could speak to him personally, Esther thought. Perhaps then she could understand his distress. Had something tragic happened in their street? Had something gone wrong with his work? But Mordecai would not be allowed any nearer to the palace while he insisted on wearing sackcloth and wailing loudly. Esther would have to depend on Hathach to carry accurate messages back and forth until the problem could be sorted out. What did that scrap of parchment mean? From what Esther could see, Mordecai's anger seemed to focus on what was written there.

At last Hathach returned.

"What is it, Hathach? What is my uncle so upset about?"

"It is the king's new law, my queen," the servant said humbly.

"What law? The king makes laws every day. What is special about this one?"

"Your uncle says that Haman has organized a plan to destroy the Jewish people, and the king has given his consent."

"Destroy the Jewish people?" Esther echoed in disbelief. "Why would my husband make such an order? The Jews have not been troublesome to his kingdom."

"I cannot say, my queen. But the decree has been sealed with the royal ring and sent out to all the provinces. Mordecai has a copy. I saw it for myself. On a certain day, it will be lawful for Persians to kill the Jews and plunder their goods."

Now Esther fully understood Mordecai's distress. Four years had passed since she had been made queen, and still Xerxes did not know that she was Jewish. If he had known, would it have influenced his decision? Surely she would be safe within the palace—but what about Mordecai? She knew Haman hated her uncle. Mordecai's life was certainly in danger.

"I have none of the king's power, Hathach," Esther said. "What does my uncle think I can do?"

"He begs you to go to the king and beg for mercy for the Jewish people."

"But if the decree has been sealed with the royal ring, then it has already been made law. I cannot change that!"

Hathach was silent, knowing that his role was merely that of a servant and a messenger, not an advisor to the queen. Esther wished he would speak, but he did not. She grieved for what would happen to Mordecai and the rest of her people. But what could she possibly do? She had no authority to reverse his decree, and she felt she would have very little influence on his decision.

"This is what I want you to tell my uncle," Esther said at last. "Remind him that all the king's officials and the people of the royal provinces know that for any man or woman who approaches the king in the inner court without being summoned, the king has but one law: That person will be put to death. The only exception to this is for the king to extend the gold scepter and spare the person's life. But it has been more than thirty days since the king has called for me. If I go to him without being summoned, the law will apply to me also."

Esther was frightened and desperate. Perhaps Mordecai was right; perhaps she was the only hope the Jews had. But what good could she do if she were put to death?

"There must be another way! Tell Mordecai that I cannot go to the king!"

CHAPTER 6

Mordecai looked up and saw the slight figure of Esther peering out the window. There was no question that she had grown into a lovely woman, as he had always known she would. For years, he had been sad because of their separation and because Esther could not enjoy a normal life among her people. Xerxes could have had any Persian woman he wanted. Mordecai had never understood why Jewish girls had been rounded up during the search for a new queen. But now—perhaps this was exactly the reason Esther had been chosen as queen. Perhaps God Himself had done the choosing, and not merely Xerxes.

Even though she was the queen and lived inside the palace, Esther did not always know very much about the king's business, especially where Haman was involved. So it was quite possible that she truly did not know about the new law and the reason why Mordecai was wailing in the street. When she found out what was written on the parchment he held tightly in his hand, she would be as angry as he was. He was sure of that. Although she had not lived among the Jews for nearly eight years now, Mordecai simply could not believe that Esther would turn her back on them. Surely once she understood the seriousness of the circumstances, she would do everything in her power to save her own people.

When Hathach returned with Esther's message saying

that she could not go to the king, Mordecai listened carefully and then raised his eyes toward Esther's window in disbelief and disappointment. For a moment he was overcome with helplessness and personal sorrow. Esther had allowed her own fear to rob her of the courage she needed to rise to this challenge. But Mordecai would not give up.

"I have one more message for the queen, Hathach. Listen carefully, and give her this message exactly: Do not think that because you are in the king's house you alone of all the Jews will escape. For if you remain silent at this time, relief and deliverance for the Jews will arrive from another place, but you and your father's family will perish. And who knows but that you have come to royal position for such a time as this?"

"What does he mean, Hathach?" Esther demanded when she received Mordecai's message.

"It is not for me to say, my queen. I have given you the message exactly as it was given to me. I can do no more."

"Of course not. Please wait outside my door. I will call you when I have prepared an answer for my uncle."

Esther was left alone in her room. She looked around at the luxury that surrounded her: more clothes than she would ever wear, the most expensive perfumes, cosmetic creams to keep her youthful and lovely, a choice of couches for lounging or eating when trays of gourmet foods were carried in to her by one of the many servants who waited on her every moment of the day. Heavy, full drapes with delicately twisted gold braid adorned her windows. She slept on a bed filled with the softest feathers and covered with the finest fabrics in the kingdom. If she wanted something, she simply rang a bell and a servant appeared to satisfy her wish. She was respected and honored as the queen by everyone in the palace.

Yet Mordecai's message implied that even she would not be safe inside the palace. He was right, of course. Although the king himself did not know she was Jewish, many other people did. She could not be certain she would survive the day that the decree was carried out.

It struck her that she had nothing to lose by approaching the king. He might order her death, but she would surely lose her life in a few months anyway. And if he extended the gold scepter to her—she might be able to find a way to help her people. Perhaps now was the time to tell Xerxes that she was among the people he had ordered killed. She had nothing to lose and everything to gain—for herself and her people.

She spun around and raced to her door, calling, "Hathach! Hathach!"

The servant appeared promptly, eager to do as she asked.

"Tell Mordecai this," she said triumphantly. "Go, gather together all the Jews who are in Susa and fast for me. Do not eat or drink for three days, night or day. I and my maids will fast as you do. When this is done, I will go to the king, even though it is against the law. And if I perish, I perish."

Esther ran back to the window and watched as her message was delivered. A smile began to cross Mordecai's face, and then it broke into a full grin. He looked up at her with pride and gratitude beaming from his features. Then she knew she had made the right choice.

Just as she instructed, for three days and three nights, Esther and her maids and all Jewish people in the city of Susa had nothing to eat or drink. They prayed constantly for Esther and the challenge she was about to face. Everyone understood how important it was to all of them for the queen to succeed.

Esther had many moments of doubt and fear. More than once she was tempted to send a message to Mordecai saying that she could not carry out her promise. When she slept, she dreamed of the moment when she would approach the king. Sometimes in her dream he would hold out the gold scepter in approval; other times he did not, and she would wake up screaming with terror. During the day Esther sat in her high window looking out into the streets. She did not know many people in the city anymore, but she knew that many of them were Jews whose lives were in danger. She prayed harder and more intensely for courage and strength.

On the third morning, Esther dressed carefully. She had made thorough preparations for this day. The time had come when she was thankful for her exquisite beauty. Perhaps it would be her loveliness that would make the king extend his scepter and welcome her into his presence when he had not called for her. She put on her finest royal robes and used the perfume that she knew Xerxes liked. Trembling with every step she took, she walked through the palace and stood in the inner court, where King Xerxes was sitting on his throne. It was dangerous enough to be there at all; she could not risk speaking. She would have to wait until he looked up and saw her standing there and hope that he would be pleased with what he saw.

Esther tried to smile and look relaxed, but her eyes were drawn to the gold scepter at the king's side. She was startled when Xerxes looked up and spoke.

"Queen Esther! I do not remember that I called for you."

Esther was still watching the gold scepter. It did not move.

Esther held her breath for what seemed like hours, waiting to see if Xerxes would lift his scepter and point it toward her.

At last his hand moved toward his side, and she saw the glint of gold as the scepter was raised. To her relief, the expression on his face was soft and gentle.

"What is it, Queen Esther?" he asked. "What is your request? I will give you up to half my kingdom."

Xerxes had said those words to Esther many times in the four years they had been married. Never had she asked anything of him, and certainly not half his kingdom! In the three days she had spent fasting and praying, she had pictured this moment in her mind often. What would she say to the king? Was this the right moment to reveal her Jewish background? Should she fall on her face and beg for mercy? She had planned what she would say, but all of a sudden she wanted to turn around and run from the room.

Esther swallowed once and tried to speak. Her voice hardly sounded like it was hers, but the words she heard were the ones she had rehearsed. "If it pleases the king," she said, "let the king, together with Haman, come today to a banquet I have prepared for him."

The king smiled widely. "A banquet with my lovely queen —what a wonderful idea. I have been so busy with the affairs of the kingdom that I have not seen my wife for weeks."

Xerxes turned to the servant standing near him. "Bring Haman at once, so that we may do what Esther asks."

The king stood up and offered his arm to Esther. She smiled and laid her hand on his arm, and they left the room together.

When they entered the banquet hall, the queen once again held her breath while she waited for the king's reaction. She had planned an elaborate banquet with fine meats, fresh breads, juicy fruits, and crisp vegetables. Everything was laid out attractively on a long table covered with a sparkling white linen tablecloth. There was much more food than three people could possibly eat in one day. The colors and textures of the foods blended together perfectly, like an artist's painting, and the fragrances rising from the steaming dishes were irresistible. Three low couches covered with silk in regal colors were grouped in front of the table for Xerxes, Esther, and Haman to lounge on while they enjoyed the feast. A dozen servants stood ready to serve them on gold plates and wine goblets.

"You have done well, Queen Esther," said Xerxes. "I will be pleased to sit at your banquet."

Esther smiled in relief and began to relax. By the time Haman entered the room, she felt confident that her plan might indeed work. She would please the king in every way possible, even including Haman in the festivities, and then she would make her request on behalf of her people.

The three of them feasted for nearly three hours. Servants brought to them a steady stream of fresh plates heaped with a wide variety of food and poured wine freely from the many jugs Esther had arranged for. Xerxes and Haman talked at length about business matters, while Esther smiled and made sure that the king continued to be pleased. She was alert for any mention of Haman's cruel plan against the Jews, but it was not discussed. Often she felt Haman looking at her in an odd way. She met his gaze with ease and confidence, but she could not help wondering what he was thinking about. Was he planning how he would kill her along with Mordecai? Was he suspicious about why she had invited him to this special banquet?

At last Xerxes turned his attention to Esther. He reached for her slender hand and pulled her to his side.

"Now what is it you really want, Esther?" he asked. "Surely you did not risk coming into the inner court without being called simply to invite me to a banquet. Whatever you want, I will give it to you, up to half of my kingdom."

The moment had come for Esther to decide what to say. Haman was looking at her. Clearly he was also very curious about what Esther's words might be. In a fleeting moment, Esther had to judge the king's state of mind and answer his question.

"My petition and request is this," she said. "If the king regards me with favor and it pleases the king to grant my petition and fulfill my request, let the king and Haman come tomorrow to the banquet I will prepare for them. Then I will answer the king's question."

"Very well," said Xerxes. "You make me very curious,

Queen Esther. This has been a wonderful banquet today, and I will look forward to another exquisite feast tomorrow."

Haman bowed his head to Esther. "I am flattered that the queen would invite me to a banquet such as this. I will be honored to be the queen's guest once again tomorrow."

The two men left the banquet hall. Esther let out a sigh and collapsed back onto her couch. Although the room was very warm, she was trembling. What would happen if the king changed his mind and did not come to her banquet tomorrow? Had she missed her chance to speak to him about what was really on her mind? Had she made the wrong choice when she decided to wait another day?

Esther refused to let her fear overcome her. She had promised Mordecai she would speak to the king on behalf of her people. As frightened as she was, she knew that she was the one person in the kingdom who was in a position to help the Jews.

Abruptly, she stood up and called the servants in the room to her. "We will make another banquet for the king tomorrow," she said. "It will be even more beautiful than today, with more of the king's favorite foods. I will select the food myself. We will have the royal musicians come in and play music that pleases the king. If the king wishes to dance, we will dance."

The rest of the day was spent planning for the second banquet. At last, weary from a busy day, Esther returned to her own room. Out of habit, she moved to the window and looked out. She had not seen Mordecai during the three days of fasting and praying, and she did not really expect to see him now. Nevertheless, she longed to sit with him as she had when she was a little girl and feel the comfort that would come from his presence.

The streets were quiet at the end of the day. Esther thought of her own little street in the Jewish corner of the city and wished that she could once again move freely from house to house with Rebekah and her other friends. But those days were gone. And after all these years of life in the palace, Esther was beginning to understand that there was a reason why she had been taken from the marketplace that morning eight years earlier.

CHAPTER 8

Haman left the palace whistling that day. What a feast! And what an honor to have been invited to dine alone with the royal couple. If the queen herself showed him such respect, he surely deserved the honor of the other royal officials kneeling down when he passed by. When he walked through the gate, Haman nodded at the officers who had replaced Bigthana and Teresh. Nearby was Mordecai, just finishing his work for the day. Haman paused slightly to give Mordecai an opportunity to honor him.

Mordecai lifted his eyes briefly, then went about his business without acknowledging Haman's presence. Immediately Haman's good mood disappeared and he was filled with rage. No matter what other honors he received, he was overcome with anger whenever he thought of Mordecai and how this one man refused to bow to him. Haman held his tongue, however. The king's decree had been sent to all the provinces, and Haman would have his revenge in only a few months.

Haman strolled the streets to his spacious, luxurious home in a wealthy part of Susa. He was greeted by his wife, Zeresh, and several friends who were visiting.

"Our meal will be ready in a few minutes, Haman," Zeresh said. "I have instructed the servants to prepare your favorite foods tonight."

"My dear wife, I am afraid I have no appetite," Haman answered.

"But why not?"

Haman lifted his head proudly. "I have been to a banquet hosted by the queen."

Zeresh shrugged her shoulders. "You have been to many royal banquets."

"That's right," said one of Haman's friends. "You are always boasting to us about the exotic food you eat at the palace."

Haman smiled. "This one was different. This was a very private meal. The king and I were the only guests invited by the queen."

Haman looked around and saw that his wife and guests were impressed.

"My career has been successful beyond any dreams I ever had," Haman bragged. "In only a few short years, the king has promoted me above all the other royal officials and trusted me with important responsibilities. He discusses things with me that he talks about to no one else. It is almost as if we are ruling the kingdom together."

"You have worked very hard, my husband," Zeresh said. "You have deserved every honor you have received."

"The king has even trusted me with his signet ring. I have the authority to declare laws in his name."

"Haman, I have known you for many years," said his friend. "You have always been very fair. The king is wise to trust you. It was only fitting that he should command the other officials to pay honor to you."

The smile was wiped from Haman's face and replaced by a scowl.

"I would be a happy man if it were not for that Jew, Mordecai," he said. "The king has honored me; the queen has invited me to another banquet tomorrow. Yet I am not satisfied because when I walk past Mordecai, he refuses to acknowledge my position. I cannot stand to see him at the king's gate, acting as if he were more important than I am."

"Then why don't you do something about it?" Zeresh said.

"Yes," said their friend. "You just said you had the authority of the king's ring. Why not go to the king tomorrow morning and ask that Mordecai be hanged? Then you can enjoy your banquet with the queen without thinking about that man ever again."

Haman was nodding. Perhaps this was a good idea. He would not have to wait until the day his new law would be carried out. Mordecai was openly disobeying the king's command to honor Haman. This was already against the law, so why not have him hanged now?

"You can have the gallows built tonight," his wife suggested. "Make it very high—seventy-five feet—so that everyone can see what happens to a man who does not honor my worthy husband."

Haman's face showed his pleasure once again. "You are true friends and a dear wife. I will do as you have suggested. Please, go in and dine on the meal my wife has prepared. I will take care of the details of the gallows and join you later."

CHAPTER 9

Xerxes could not sleep.

He punched at his pillows, threw the covers off, pulled them back on again, turned over to his back, laid on one side, then the other—nothing worked. He simply could not sleep that night. Perhaps it was too much rich food from Esther's banquet keeping him awake. Whatever the reason for his sleeplessness, it was very late when he grew frustrated and rang the bell for his personal attendant to come.

The servant entered with a lamp in his hand. "What is the king's wish?"

"I cannot sleep. Go find the official records of my reign and read to me."

The attendant read for hours and hours. Although he was having difficulty staying awake himself, the king showed no signs of going to sleep, so the reading continued. They came to the portion of the official record that retold the story of how Mordecai had exposed Bigthana and Teresh, the guards who had plotted to kill the king.

The king was sitting upright, wide awake. He had completely forgotten about this incident until now. As the attendant began to read about another subject, King Xerxes interrupted.

"What honor and recognition has Mordecai received for this?" he asked.

The servant looked again at the writing in front of him,

searching for an answer to the king's question. "Nothing has been done for him."

Xerxes got out of bed and glanced toward the window, where daylight was peeking in. "Who is in the court this morning?"

The attendant hurriedly asked another servant. "I am told that Haman has just arrived, my king," he said. "He was hoping to have a word with you this morning."

"Bring him in," Xerxes ordered.

Haman entered very quickly, pleased that the king had agreed to see him so early in the morning and in his private chambers.

"Haman," Xerxes said, "what should be done for the man the king delights to honor?"

Of course, he means me, Haman thought to himself. *I will wait to speak to him about Mordecai another day.* He thought carefully before he spoke. Perhaps if he asked for something other than wealth, the king would be flattered. Aloud, Haman said, "For the man the king delights to honor have them bring a royal robe the king has worn and a horse the king has ridden, one with a royal crest placed on its head. Then let the robe and horse be entrusted to one of the king's most noble princes. Let them robe the man the king delights to honor, and lead him on the horse through the city streets proclaiming before him, 'This is what is done for the man the king delights to honor.' "

Haman was already picturing himself astride a royal horse, wearing a robe that the king himself had worn. For a moment, he was able to forget about Mordecai and enjoy the honor the king intended to give him.

"Go at once," the king commanded Haman. "Get the robe and the horse and do just as you have suggested. Do this for Mordecai the Jew, who sits at the king's gate. Be sure not to neglect anything you have recommended. It is a perfect plan."

Haman hardly knew what to say. "Yes, my king." The thought of having to honor Mordecai made him feel sick. He wondered what he had done to displease the king that would make him deserve this humiliation.

Xerxes sighed contentedly. "I have been up all night, Haman, but I believe I can sleep now. Don't forget about Queen Esther's banquet. I will see you there."

Haman had been dismissed. But there were witnesses to what the king had commanded. Haman had no choice but to carry out the plan he had described when he thought he was the one to be honored.

Angrily, Haman went to the king's dressing room and selected a royal robe, one which he had seen the king wearing only a few days ago. He carried this with him to the royal stables and chose a horse that the king had ridden only once. The crest that indicated that this was the king's horse was placed on the animal's head, and Haman led the way to where he knew he would find Mordecai.

Mordecai looked up from his work. "Haman, even with a horse and a royal crest, you are not worthy of my honor."

A crowd had gathered at the unusual sight of Haman standing before Mordecai with one of the king's horses. Haman heard some snickering from deep within the crowd but forced himself not to turn around and look.

"The horse is for you, Mordecai, along with this royal robe sent from King Xerxes for you to wear."

"Is this some kind of joke, Haman?" Mordecai demanded. "Why would the king send a horse and a robe for me to wear? I have never even spoken to him."

"Apparently he believes you saved his life." Haman had to force out every word.

"So I did," said Mordecai with conviction.

"The king wishes to honor you for that deed." Haman held open the robe for Mordecai.

Mordecai was still not sure what to believe. After a brief hesitation, he stepped forward and allowed Haman to wrap the robe around him and help him mount the horse. To Mordecai's surprise, Haman himself took the reins of the horse and led him through the streets. On every block, he cried out, "This is what is done for the man the king delights to honor."

A crowd gathered on nearly every corner. Haman and Mordecai were both well-known men, and their hatred for each other had been obvious for a long time. Cheers and boos were heard in response to the sight of the king's highest official leading the horse of a Jew.

At last, completely humiliated, Haman returned Mordecai to his place outside the palace. Haman himself ran home as quickly as he could.

"What is it, Haman?" asked Zeresh, alarmed that her husband should come home in the middle of the day. "You look terrible! What happened to you?"

"Haman, my friend," said his guest, "you are covered with dust and sweat. What in the world have you been doing?"

Haman covered his face in shame and grief. He did not answer their questions for a long time. But he knew that word would reach them soon enough, so he began to tell them what had happened that morning.

"I went to the palace early to see the king, as you suggested," he said. "I was delighted when he called me into his private chambers. But before I could ask his permission to hang Mordecai, the king was asking me what should be done to a man the king wished to honor."

Haman stopped and shook his head sadly. "I have been such a fool. I thought he meant me! I thought he wanted to give me further honor, so I suggested a royal robe and a royal horse. Then I found out he meant Mordecai! I went to see the king this morning because I wanted to hang Modecai for not honoring me. Instead, the king ordered me to honor Mordecai by walking through the streets while Mordecai rode a royal horse. The whole city has seen me. I am ruined!"

The once proud Haman collapsed on a couch and covered his face with his hands. "How can I possibly go back and face the king now? I will not be able to walk through the streets without people sneering at me."

Sadly, Zeresh agreed. "You have been publicly humiliated by a Jew. If only you had spoken to the king sooner about Mordecai—this would never have happened."

Haman, Zeresh, and their guests sat together in silence,

sharing the grief of the official's shame. After a long time, they were interrupted by the soft knock of a servant.

"Yes?" said Zeresh.

"The king's servant has arrived to remind Haman of the queen's banquet."

Haman once again hid his face in his hands.

CHAPTER 10

Esther was ready for Haman and Xerxes to enter the banquet hall. She had slept very little the night before. Instead, she had spent the hours praying and begging God for courage and mercy. Still nervous about what she faced, she felt more brave than she had since she first committed herself to this plan.

She moved through the hall inspecting the preparations and was very satisfied. The gold plates and goblets sparkled in the bright light coming in through the windows. Fresh flowers from the palace gardens adorned the tables. The food had been prepared perfectly. She had made sure that everything that the king liked best was on the menu and prepared personally by the chief palace cook. Skilled musicians stood by with trumpets and lyres to fill the hall with the king's favorite music. The couches were lined with soft pillows for the king's comfort, and the servants were ready to do whatever the queen directed.

When Haman arrived, Esther thought that he looked very tired. She had not heard about the embarrassment he had suffered that morning, but she sensed that something was wrong with him. He seemed even more eager than usual to please King Xerxes, but Esther did not believe that his smile was sincere. Yesterday he had been lighthearted and proud. Today, he acted very nervous and discouraged.

The meal went very well. To Esther's relief, the king

seemed pleased with everything she had selected and ate heartily. Xerxes and Haman joked and laughed together, and the king often smiled at his wife as they spent the entire afternoon eating. Esther was nervous, but she felt encouraged that the feast was going so well. Haman was acting a bit odd, she thought, but she could not be distracted by worrying about the king's high official. There was a purpose for this banquet, and she must remember it at every moment.

At the end of the meal, when none of them could eat anything more, the king signaled for more wine and settled back comfortably on his couch.

"And now, my queen," Xerxes said, "you must tell me about your request. You may have anything you wish, up to half of my kingdom."

Esther knew the moment had come; she could delay no further. Everything had gone according to plan up to this point, and she prayed quickly and silently that what she was about to say would be well received by the king.

"If I have found favor with you, O king, and if it pleases your majesty, grant me my life—this is my petition. And spare my people—this is my request." Esther kept her eyes fixed on Xerxes as she spoke, resisting the temptation to look at Haman for his reaction. "For I and my people have been sold for destruction and slaughter and annihilation. If we had merely been sold as male and female slaves, I would have kept quiet, because that would not justify disturbing the king."

Xerxes sat up straight on the edge of his couch. "What are you talking about, Queen Esther? What do you mean, you have been sold for destruction and slaughter?"

"I am Jewish, O king."

The king continued to look puzzled.

"A law has been issued with the king's signet ring to destroy my people."

"Who has done this?" Xerxes demanded. "Where is the man who has dared to do such a thing?"

Esther now turned her head toward Haman. She struggled to keep her voice from breaking. "Our enemy is this man, Haman."

"The Jews, Haman?" Xerxes shouted. "You want to destroy the Jews? You told me there were people who would be a threat to my power. The Jews are no such threat!"

Haman was visibly frightened. He, too, was sitting on the edge of his couch. He stuttered as he began to speak. "I. . . I. . .I was only trying to do what is best for the kingdom, your majesty."

"You tricked me! You used my signet ring for your own purposes, and now this horrible idea has been made law."

Esther had never seen the king so angry. His eyes bulged, and his face was flaming red. His loud shouting echoed throughout the banquet hall, and the sound magnified his rage. The servants, who had been quietly clearing the table, now stood very still as they watched the king. Xerxes stomped over to the table and set his wine goblet down very hard. Then he turned on his heel and left the hall through the door that led to the palace gardens, his royal robes flapping briskly behind him.

For a very long moment, Esther and Haman stared at each other while a dozen servants looked on. No one in the room moved.

Encouraged by the king's anger, Esther now felt she had the upper hand. She straightened her shoulders and spoke confidently. "I believe our banquet has come to an end, Haman. You may leave. I am sure the king will call for you when he is ready to see you."

Haman lurched toward Esther. "Queen Esther, this has all been a misunderstanding," he said. "Please allow me to explain. . . ."

Esther put up her hand to stop Haman. "You will come no closer to the queen."

"I am begging for my life, my queen. You alone can spare me." Haman was very desperate and looked as if he might even cry. "I plead for your royal mercy, Queen Esther. Spare my life."

Esther looked at Haman without sympathy. "I know that you hate my uncle, Haman. In fact, you hate all my people, even me. How is it that you, who have no mercy in you, should dare to plead with the queen for mercy for your own life?"

Although she was very tense about this encounter with Haman, Esther had remained on her couch, trying to appear in control. Haman once again moved toward her—and this time he lost his balance and toppled on top of the queen.

"Get off!" she screamed. "How dare you!" Then she heard an angry shout.

"Haman!" King Xerxes had entered the banquet hall

once again, just as Haman fell on top of Esther. He rushed across the empty room and roughly grabbed Haman by the hair and pulled him off Esther. He turned the official around and roared directly into his face. "Will you even stoop so low as to attack the queen? You are a greater fool than I, Haman. Get out of my sight!"

King Xerxes pushed Haman into the waiting arms of soldiers who had followed the king in and now had their swords drawn, standing ready for the king's command. It was obvious to all that Haman was doomed to die.

The king's personal attendant, who had served Xerxes for many years, stepped forward to speak to the king. "Your majesty, if it please the king, Haman has this very morning built a high gallows at his own home. He was intending to hang Mordecai, the Jew."

"Hang him on it," Xerxes thundered.

CHAPTER 11

"I did it, Uncle! I did it!" Esther rushed excitedly into Mordecai's arms as if she were a little girl. "Haman will cause us no more trouble. Now that the king knows you are my uncle, you will be welcome in the palace whenever we want to see each other."

Mordecai laughed at Esther's excitement. "I am very proud of my beautiful niece! I was confident at every moment that you would do the right thing."

They sat together in the palace gardens, one of Esther's favorite places. Mordecai had never been permitted to come to this part of the palace before, but he could see now why Esther loved to sit in the garden. It was truly lovely and very restful. He hoped that they would have many more visits in this pleasant setting.

Esther laid her head on Mordecai's shoulder. "I am so glad that ordeal is over," she said. "I'm not sure I could have held on much longer. Just being in the same room with Haman made me so nervous!"

"My dear niece, you did a wonderful job," Mordecai said proudly. "Without your courage, our people would be without hope. But the ordeal is not over. It has only begun."

Abruptly, Esther sat up and looked her uncle in the face. "What do you mean, Uncle?"

Mordecai spoke calmly and quietly. "Esther, you have

grown up under Persian rule. I am sure you know the nature of Persian law."

For a moment, Esther did not speak. Then she put into words what her uncle had reminded her of. "Once a decree has been made into law, it cannot be reversed."

"That is correct," Mordecai said sadly. "Haman may be gone, but his plan remains law. Our people still face the day of execution."

"But I spoke to the king. . . ," Esther protested.

Mordecai interrupted her. "Even the king cannot reverse a law."

"Then what more can we do?" Esther asked desperately. "We are no better off than before."

"You must speak to the king again, Esther."

"For what purpose, Uncle?"

"The king cannot change the law, but he can make a new decree that would allow us to defend ourselves."

Esther shook her head sadly. "There will still be a great deal of Jewish bloodshed."

Mordecai nodded. "Perhaps. Or it might be that the knowledge that we are prepared to defend ourselves will discourage our attackers from doing as Haman wished."

"You are very wise, Uncle. Why my husband chose to promote Haman and not you is something I do not understand."

Mordecai smiled. "And you are very sweet. But we must find a way to speak to the king. Do you think he will call for you soon?"

"I never know. After what happened with Haman, perhaps

he will want to see me again very soon."

"My queen," said the voice of a servant behind them.

Esther turned her head. "Yes?"

"The king wishes to see you in the inner court. He asks that your uncle come with you."

Esther and Mordecai looked at each other and grinned.

"This is your opportunity," Mordecai urged. "It would not be proper for me to speak to the king on this subject, but perhaps he would listen to his queen."

In the throne room, Xerxes greeted Esther and Mordecai warmly. "Do not be alarmed. I wish to welcome you and honor you for your deeds."

Mordecai bowed deeply before the king. "I am most honored to be in your presence. Allow me to express my gratitude for the royal robe and the royal horse presented to me earlier today."

"What a wonderful and terrible day we have all had," the king said. "In the morning, Mordecai was honored because he saved my life. In the afternoon, Haman, my most trusted official, was hanged because he wished to destroy your people." The king turned to Esther. "I believe it would be proper for you to have Haman's property, Queen Esther. This represents a great deal of money. I am sure you will find a wise use for it."

"Thank you, your majesty. If it pleases the king, I wish for my uncle to be given charge over the money. He is more wise than I could ever hope to be."

"Very well. I will make the arrangements." Now Xerxes turned to Mordecai. "I have something else for you, Mordecai, something of far greater significance than a horse or a robe."

King Xerxes held up his signet ring and motioned for Mordecai to step forward to receive it. "I have trusted the wrong man for many years. From now on, I will trust the right man. Mordecai shall wear the signet ring, which represents my authority."

Once again, Mordecai bowed deeply. He was overcome with shock that the king should make such a gesture toward him. As he rose to his feet again, Mordecai glanced at Esther and tried to use his eyes to urge her to speak to the king about Haman's decree.

Esther took her cue from her uncle. She fell before the king and began to weep. Immediately Xerxes stooped down and lifted her to her feet again. "My queen, what should cause you such distress? You have just been greatly honored, and I have raised your uncle to an important position in my kingdom. Why do you weep?"

"If it pleases the king," Esther said, "and if he regards me with favor and thinks it is the right thing to do, and if he is pleased with me, let an order be written to overturn the law that Haman sent to all the provinces for the destruction of the Jews. For how can I bear to see such disaster fall on my people? How can I bear to see the destruction of my family?"

"I have already given this much thought, Queen Esther," the king assured her. "No document written in the king's name and sealed with his ring can be reversed. But we can write a new document." He turned to Mordecai. "I will leave it to your judgment to determine what this new document must say in order to protect your people. You may use the royal secretaries to write it and the couriers to carry it to the far corners of my kingdom. Use the signet ring I have given you, and this document shall also become law."

The royal secretaries were called in immediately, and Mordecai set them to work very quickly. He had already planned what the document must say. The Jews in every city of the kingdom would have the right to band together and defend themselves against their enemies on the day that Haman had chosen to attack the Jews. They could form their own armies to protect their families and property from any armies that might attack them. Esther was right; there would be bloodshed, but at least the Jews would have the right to defend themselves.

Mordecai's new law was sent to every province in the kingdom. As the couriers left on their journeys, Mordecai looked on with deep satisfaction. His own rise in power was meaningless to him. The royal robes and the crown that the king had placed on his head were not important. His satisfaction came from knowing that Esther would be safe and that instead of wailing and grieving, there would be joy and gladness among the Jews throughout the kingdom.

CHAPTER 12

"What are you working on, Uncle?" Esther walked happily into the room in the palace where her uncle now spent his days working for the king. She opened the drapes on the window to let in some fresh air. "Why do you always forget to open the windows when you come into this room?" she chided. "It's so much more pleasant when you let in some light and air."

Mordecai shrugged his shoulders. "I suppose I'm too busy. There is always so much work to do. I just never think about it." He put down his quill and rubbed his eyes with the heels of his hands. He had stayed at his writing table very late last night and had returned very early in the morning.

Eighteen months had passed since the final encounter with Haman. Even the awful day of destruction was behind them now. The Jews had organized and prepared well; they had been the victors in the skirmishes and battles that occurred throughout the kingdom. Many more Persians were killed than Jews. Mordecai and Esther had been protected within the walls of the palace and guarded closely against any possible attack.

Xerxes had been very pleased with everything Mordecai had done for him during the months since Haman's plot had been overthrown. Esther's humble uncle was rapidly taking on more authority and responsibility in the kingdom.

Esther walked over to the table where her uncle was bent

over a parchment, once again intent on his writing. Although he was concentrating, she did not hesitate to interrupt. She knew he was always glad to see her, no matter how busy he was.

"I'm so glad we can be together in the palace now, Uncle. I know we can never get back the eight years we were apart, but it is wonderful to be able to see you every day."

Mordecai smiled in agreement. "It is because of you that we are together now—because you were willing to face an enormous challenge."

"I would never have done it if the challenge had not come from you, Uncle. I knew that if you thought I should do it, then it was the right thing."

"God was gracious to our people. He heard our prayers and answered our cries. We were honored to be His instruments."

Esther nodded. Her uncle expressed exactly what she felt. After a moment she repeated the question she had asked when she entered the room. "What are you working on?" She leaned over his shoulder to look at the parchment.

"I am very relieved to have Haman's wicked plan completely behind us," Mordecai answered. "But one thing still bothers me. If we try to forget the terrible part of those days, we will also forget the wonderful part. I do not want our people to forget the ordeal that we faced. We were victorious on the day of destruction planned by Haman, and we rejoice in God's deliverance." He gestured toward the words he had written. "I want all Jews throughout the kingdom to teach their children this story, so I am writing it down before I become too old to remember everything that happened. We must always remember the day that our sorrow was turned into joy, and the time that our mourning was changed into celebration."

Esther gently stroked her uncle's head. "Do you mean a feast, Uncle? Shall we have a feast to remember this deliverance, just as we celebrated the deliverance of the Passover when our people left Egypt?"

Mordecai was pleased with Esther's response. "That's exactly what I mean," he said enthusiastically. "I want us to have a holiday every year, two days of feasting and giving presents of food to one another and gifts to the poor. Every year on the anniversary of the day that Haman chose by casting lots, we will remember that our lives do not belong to those who use the pur to make decisions. We are still God's people."

He paused and turned around in his chair. His face was bright with conviction.

"Esther, for many years, we did not understand why you had been taken from us or why you had been chosen as queen," Mordecai continued. "You always used to say that you would rather have married a Jewish man and lived a normal life. But when our day of destruction was upon us, then I knew that God Himself had placed you in the palace. What seemed like bad luck to us was really part of God's plan."

Once again Esther simply nodded. She loved seeing her uncle so excited, and his idea was exciting to her, as well. "Do you have a name for the holiday?"

Mordecai lifted the parchment for Esther to see for her-self. "It shall be called Purim,[2] to remind us that even when things seem to happen by chance, we are still within God's control. Our God is truly a great God!"

---

[2] Jewish people everywhere still celebrate Purim, the Feast of Lots, usually in mid-March.

MARY

MOTHER OF JESUS

by Ellyn Sanna

CHAPTER 1

Fifteen-year-old Mary ran up the path that led out of Nazareth, a water bucket swinging from her arm. She skimmed past the small, dusty houses, her stomach full of excited butterflies. The sun was already sinking low in the sky, and she was in a hurry to reach the well where she would draw the water for the evening meal. Joseph would be eating with her family tonight.

She had promised to marry him in a year's time, but she was still a little shy around him. Their time together was short, and they seldom had a chance to speak alone. Each time she saw him, though, she loved him more. She hoped he felt the same about her.

Tonight she wanted to get back from the well in time to wash her face and arms, for she had been helping Ema, her mother, grind wheat all day, and she knew the fine, pale dust still clung to her skin. She did not want Joseph to see her looking grimy and sweat-streaked.

As she climbed the hill out of town, however, her feet slowed. This was her favorite time to come to the well, when most of the other women would be busy in their own homes preparing the evening meals, and Mary could walk alone, looking at the sky and the fields and the blue hills that lay along the horizon like smoke. She seldom had a chance to be by herself, but here on the empty path, with only the sound of the quiet wind murmuring through the grass, she had a chance to think and examine her heart. Here, she could open herself to God.

Long ago, when Mary was only a small child, her mother had said to her, "You have to choose, Mary. Do you want your own way? Or do you want God's way?"

Mary smiled, remembering. She had been so angry that day, and she hadn't wanted Ema to start talking about God. But her mother had bent over the bread she was kneading, pressing her fingers deep into the soft dough, and then she had said, "When we accept everything that happens to us—even the things that anger us or make us sad—as gifts from God's hands, then He can use everything that happens to us for His purposes. Everything—the little things and the big things, the good things and the things that seem too hard for us to bear."

Ema's strong hands paused, and she looked up over the flat rooftop of their home. She sighed, her face troubled. "Some things are hard, even when you're grown. Look at your cousin Elizabeth who visited us last week. All her life she has prayed for a child of her own. And all this time, again and again, God tells her no. And yet Elizabeth never stops saying yes to God's will, even when she longs for something different. Even when the other women point at her and whisper because she has no children."

Ema's face cleared, and she smiled as she shaped the dough into a round ball. "Our God knows what is best for us. You will be surprised, Mary, how simply saying yes to God can change everything."

Mary had not understood exactly what Ema had been saying that day. Her cousin Elizabeth was much older than she was, older even than Ema, and Elizabeth's problems had not seemed as important as Mary's own. But that night when her father taught his children from the Torah and the Psalms, Mary had heard the words in a new way.

Now, as Mary reached the well, she gave a sigh of contentment, glad that no one else was there, no women gossiping about their neighbors, none of her friends giggling over the young men. For once the stone well stood empty on the high plain. Mary leaned against the windswept cedar tree, remembering again the words her father had said on that long-ago night.

"The God of Israel and the God of David is your God, too, children," Abba had told them, his deep voice gentle and full of joy. "We are His people and the sheep of His pasture. Because He is your shepherd, you will always have everything that you need. You will live in the house of the Lord forever."

His words had been like a door opening wide in her heart. God was as real as Abba and Ema. . .and He loved her! The knowledge made goose bumps prick her skin.

After that, she liked to pretend that everywhere she went was God's house, each place a different room in an endless mansion. And she practiced saying yes to God every day, over and over again. Sometimes she found she could say yes to big things easier than she could to little things—but she discovered that each yes she said opened her heart that much wider to God and His love. If she said yes often enough, she reasoned, one day she would have a space inside her that would be big enough to be another room in God's great mansion. . . .

Mary glanced at the sun sinking lower in the west. She pushed the memories out of her head and leaned over the well. The cool, dark hole smelled like rain and stones, and Mary had always loved to peer down into its depth, looking for the blue glimmer of the sky's reflection far, far below. Today as she dropped the bucket down, she noticed her own dusty arm, and she remembered that Joseph would be at her house soon. If she didn't hurry, he would find her covered with wheat dust. She tugged the heavy load of water upward.

Murmuring a prayer of gratitude to God for the gift of clear, sweet water, she paused a moment. Despite her need to hurry, she checked to see if there were any doors in her heart she had closed in God's face, any places where she was saying no to God instead of yes. Her life was full of good gifts lately, things to which she could easily say yes—like Joseph. She smiled to herself and picked up the bucket, ready to hurry home, when a flash of light from the well stopped her. For a moment, the water in the well seemed to gleam like gold.

She bent over to peer down the dark hole, but she saw only the faint, faraway, silvery blue reflection of the evening sky. She shrugged, but as she was about to turn away, she stopped still, staring at her own arm. Each tiny mote of wheat dust that clung to the fine hairs on her skin glinted gold, making her arm shine as though it were reflecting fire.

Slowly, her heart pounding, she turned toward the source of the light. She sucked in a long, shaky breath and sank down with a thump on the edge of the well.

In front of her stood a tall, shining man dressed in white.

Chapter 2

Light poured out of him, from his skin and clothes and face; even his hair shone, she noticed. He was in the shape of a man, but she knew he was like no man she had ever seen, and his face held something for which she could find no words. . . joy and love and strength, and something more.

Her eyes traveled from his face downward, and then her heart began to pound even harder as she stared down at his feet. They were bare, as full of light as the rest of him—and they were planted firmly in the air, a good hand's breadth above the ground. Mary slid down off the stones onto her knees, her head bowed before this frightening creature.

"Greetings, favored woman!" the man said. "The Lord is with you!"

Mary kept her eyes fixed on the dusty ground beneath her knees. What do you mean? she wanted to ask. The man's words held such certainty, such joy, that she was confused. Surely he must have her confused with someone else, she thought, but when she peeked up at his face, she knew how unlikely this strange and mighty man would be to make a mistake.

"Don't be frightened, Mary," the man said.

She looked up at him. "How do you know my name?" she whispered.

The man only smiled. "God has decided to bless you!" he announced. "You will become pregnant and have a Son, and you are to name Him Jesus. He will be very great and will be called the Son of the Most High. And the Lord God will give Him the throne of His ancestor David. And He will reign over Israel forever; His Kingdom will never end!"

Mary swayed, her body trembling with terror. She put her hands flat on the ground to keep from falling on her face and stared up at the glowing man. Desperately, she tried to pay attention to the man's words—David's throne, a prince that would be born, a kingdom that would never end.

She knew that no one had sat in David's throne for hundreds of years now, and Israel had been ruled by Rome since before she was born. . .but none of that had ever been very important to her, and she could make no sense of the man's message. She grabbed at the one thing she did understand, though, and said, "How can I become pregnant? I'm not even married yet."

The man—the creature—looked down at her for a moment, his eyes filled with a stern kindness, and then he stepped around her and sat on the edge of the well. She looked at him suspiciously, but he seemed to be resting normally on the stones, not hovering in the air as he had before. He smiled. "The Holy Spirit will come upon you, and the power of the Most High will overshadow you. So the Baby born to you will be holy, and He will be called the Son of God."

"Oh." Mary still crouched on her knees on the ground, but the creature was much closer to her now, and she could not bear his radiance. She shut her eyes tight. How could he come from the same God whom she had loved and worshiped all her life? This was too strange, beyond anything she had ever thought about or imagined. His words frightened her.

The creature leaned back on his hands. "You know what else?" he asked, as casually as though he were one of her friends exchanging a bit of gossip. The crazy thought made her want to giggle, and she bit her lip and ducked her head, but not before she saw the creature smile, as though he had read her thoughts. "Your cousin Elizabeth is pregnant, too," he continued. "And she an old woman!"

His tone was so exactly like one used by the women who would gather at the well to discuss each other's business that a little piece of her giggle slipped out. The creature only nodded, his bright eyes shining. "People used to say Elizabeth would never have any children—but she's already in her sixth month."

Mary struggled to make sense of his words. Elizabeth was having a baby. But Elizabeth was old, too old to have any children now. Ema said she had given up all hope, and now that Mary was older and understood how important babies were, she felt sorry for Elizabeth, poor wrinkled woman whose life was almost over. . . .

The creature's words made no sense. If he was a messenger from God, wouldn't God have picked a more important message to send? After all, the priests always made the Lord God seem as though He were fairly busy with men's business—and here was this strange man—this creature—this angel talking about babies and pregnancies: women's business. "How can this be?" she whispered.

The angel held Mary's eyes. He reached down and picked up a small stone and held it on his flat palm. Mary looked down at the stone, wondering why he had chosen an ordinary brown pebble to hold in his shining hand—and then the stone dropped straight through the angel's hand as though his flesh weren't there at all. The pebble hit the ground and bounced, and the angel laughed, a noise so full of joy that she caught her breath. "With God nothing is impossible."

Mary's eyes were fixed on the small, brown stone that had fallen through the creature's palm. *A magician's trick,* part of her whispered stubbornly, but when she looked back up into the angel's face, she knew that this was no magician with a bunch of sleight-of-hand tricks. No, this man, this angel, lived in the house of the Lord, just as she herself did.

A rush of understanding swept through her, and she realized that God must have many rooms in His house, rooms she had never even imagined. This bright creature had come to her from one of those other rooms she had never glimpsed.

"Will you accept this gift God has given you?" the angel asked gently.

"Now?" she whispered. "Today?"

The angel nodded.

For an instant, Mary considered what it would mean for her to become pregnant now. She pictured her parents' faces, Joseph's. . . . She gasped, feeling suddenly afraid again, but she met the angel's gaze, her own eyes steady.

Love poured through her. She bowed her head, and then she spoke the word that had become so familiar to her. "Yes."

She lifted her head. "May it be done to me as you have said."

Mary didn't know how long she knelt there on the damp earth beside the well. The angel had left her, she knew, but she continued to be wrapped in an awareness of God's love, a sense of His presence stronger than any she had ever experienced. She might have spent only a moment or two there with God's Spirit; she might have spent an entire lifetime.

When she came to herself, the sun was only a red line along the western horizon. Her family would be worried about her, she knew, and she picked up the bucket of water. As she hurried down the path, the water sloshing over her hand, she realized she must have been with God, outside of time, in eternity. But how was she going to explain that to Ema and Abba? How could she explain to Joseph?

CHAPTER 3

Three weeks later, early in the morning, Mary again climbed the path that led out of Nazareth, but this time she had no bucket in her hand, and she did not stop by the well. She kept on walking, deeper and deeper into the hills.

The morning sun was bright on the fields of blue flax blossoms that grew along the path, but Mary's heart was full of shadows. Her mother and father believed her now when she said she was going to have a baby, but Ema's face was lined with worry, and Abba did his work slowly, as though his arms and legs were suddenly too heavy for him to lift.

At night when the family lay on their sleeping mats, she had heard Ema and Abba whispering, talking about her until deep into the night. She caught snatches of their words: "She is a good girl, you know she. . ." "Some man. . .a stranger. . . against her will. . ." "Could it be she spoke the truth and. . . ?" "This nonsense about Elizabeth having a baby, too. . ." "Mary does not lie. . . . She believes this story she told us. . . ." "What will Joseph. . . ?" "What shall we do?"

Each night, Mary would hear Ema's tears finally quiet, and she would hear the murmur of their prayers, and then at last their voices would be silent. But Mary would lie awake until the light of dawn came creeping through the window, her hands clasped tightly over her stomach.

During the day, she had gone about her duties quietly,

tending the chickens, helping her mother make bread, caring for her younger brothers and sisters, her heart torn between joy and sorrow. She had not spoken with Joseph since that night when she had seen the angel, the night when she had told him. If they passed each other in the street, he turned away, his face heavy with hurt and anger. She was certain he would come to her father soon and break their betrothal, leaving her to raise God's Son alone.

Each time she reached this point in her thoughts, her heart would grow tight with fear. An unmarried woman could not give birth to a child. It was against the law. . . .But no man would want her now. Why would God ask this of her?

Climbing deeper into the hills, she said softly under her breath, "Yes, God." She drew in a deep breath and squared her shoulders. "Yes," she repeated, louder this time, though her voice wobbled a little. God would provide for both her and her son. She would trust herself to God's care. "Yes," she said again, and now her voice was firm and sure.

Yesterday, a rumor had reached Nazareth from the hills where Elizabeth lived with her husband Zechariah: Elizabeth was expecting a child. When Ema heard the news, she had cried out, her voice full of joy and relief, and a little fear. Her eyes had flown to Mary. "You were right," she said slowly.

Mary nodded. "The angel told me."

"It's only a rumor," her father protested gruffly.

Last night when she lay listening to her parents' voices, she had known suddenly what she must do. The oil lamp's dim glow spilled out from the niche in the wall; Mary prayed silently in her heart while she watched the long, dark shadows flicker across the room. When her mother stepped over Mary's sleeping mat to blow out the flame, Mary caught hold of her robe.

"Ema, let me go visit Elizabeth."

Her mother crouched on the floor beside Mary. "Your father is busy with the planting now. Perhaps later, Mary."

"I want to go alone, Ema."

Her mother's hand touched her in the darkness. "It is too far for you, Mary. Especially now. . ." Her voice was troubled.

Mary sat up. "I am strong and well, Ema. And I feel the Spirit of God telling me to visit Elizabeth."

Her mother was silent for a long moment. "Very well," she said at last. "I will speak with your father."

Mary had slept peacefully last night for the first time in weeks. Her parents woke her early. They ate together quietly outside in the courtyard, their voices soft so they would not wake the other children, and then they had handed her a bag packed with food and clothing. Her father reminded her of the landmarks she must follow to reach Elizabeth and Zechariah's home. Her mother had cried. As Mary told them good-bye, their faces were full of love and worry.

Mary pushed away the memory of the lines that had creased Abba's forehead and puckered Ema's mouth. She could not take away her parents' pain. And she could not foresee the future, either. She could only say yes to God one step at a time, trusting that He would take care of everything. But sometimes saying yes was so hard to do.

When her fears had pressed in on her during the past weeks, she had hoped she might see the angel again. She would have liked the comfort of his bright face, the reassurance of his joyful voice—but he had not appeared to her again, though she lingered often at the well. Sometimes she almost wondered if she could have imagined everything that had happened. She shifted the bag over her shoulder and walked a little faster. If only Elizabeth would believe her story.

Two days later, she at last reached Zechariah and Elizabeth's small home tucked between the hills. Mary pushed her hair behind her ears and straightened her head covering. She smoothed her travel-stained robe as best she could, then took a deep breath and stuck her head inside the doorway.

"It's your cousin Mary," she called. "I've come to—"

Before she could finish, Elizabeth hurried toward her with a glad cry.

"You are favored by God above all women," she exclaimed, taking Mary's hands in hers. "Your child will be destined for God's mightiest praise."

Mary stood silent, stunned by the joy she saw in her cousin's face. After her parents' disbelief and Joseph's rejection, Elizabeth's welcome was startling, amazing. . .and comforting. Here at last was someone who believed her, someone who would rejoice with her over the angel's incredible announcement.

Elizabeth tugged her gently inside the house. "Come in. Sit down and rest. You came all that way by yourself—and in your condition, too! How are you feeling? I was very, very sick the first three months—and always hungry. Let me get you something to eat."

She turned and began bustling around, bringing out a loaf of bread and a bowl of stew, a cup of water and a portion of cheese. She glanced over her shoulder at Mary and chuckled. "You looked so shocked for a moment there when I flew at you before you could barely get a word out. Zechariah's always telling me to calm down. But this. . ." She patted her large, round belly, then waved her hand at Mary. "It's all so exciting. So amazing. I can't calm down."

She set the food in front of Mary, then sat down beside her. Her voice was soft now as she said, "I am honored that the mother of my Lord should visit me."

Mary looked at her cousin. Her hair was as white as ever, and her face was still lined, but her cheeks were as flushed as a child's, and her eyes shone. "How did you know?" Mary asked her, though anything seemed possible to her now.

Elizabeth smiled and patted her stomach again. "When you came in and greeted me, the instant I heard your voice, my baby moved in me for joy!" She leaned over and touched Mary's hand. "Go on now, Child. You need to eat. The miracle inside you is flesh and blood, remember. You'd better feed the both of you!"

While Mary ate, Elizabeth told her own story, about the angel who had come to Zechariah. Zechariah had lost his voice because he hadn't believed the angel's news, and now he could only communicate through writing. Fascinated,

Mary listened silently, but then Elizabeth wanted to know Mary's story, too. Mary took a last bite of stew, and then, shyly at first, she told Elizabeth everything that had happened. The more she told, the faster the words tumbled out of her mouth. She was so relieved to have someone who finally understood!

When she had finished, Elizabeth sat back and smiled. For a long moment, she was silent, her lips moving, and Mary knew she was praying. Then Elizabeth's smile grew wider, and she said, "You have always given your whole heart to God. You have believed that He would do what He said. That is why He has given you this wonderful blessing."

Suddenly, Mary felt as though joy was blossoming inside her, spreading wider and wider until she could no longer contain it. She burst out, "Oh, how I praise the Lord. How I rejoice in God my Savior! For He took notice of His lowly servant girl, and now generation after generation will call me blessed. For He, the Mighty One, is holy, and He has done great things for me. His mercy goes on from generation to generation, to all who fear Him. His mighty arm does tremendous things!

"How He scatters the proud and haughty ones! He has taken princes from their thrones and exalted the lowly. He has satisfied the hungry with good things and sent the rich away with empty hands.

"And how He has helped His servant Israel! He has not forgotten His promise to be merciful. For He promised our ancestors—Abraham and his children—to be merciful to them forever."

Mary understood now why she had felt God's Spirit telling her to visit Elizabeth. Surrounded by Elizabeth's delighted love and understanding, Mary could begin to prepare for the Savior's birth. She leaned back in her chair, her hands pressed against her belly, and her heart spilled over with awe and joy.

Her weeks with Elizabeth passed quickly. The age difference between them no longer seemed to matter, and the two women spent long hours talking about pregnancy and God, babies and miracles. Some evenings as they sat around the supper table, they laughed until they cried, while Zechariah listened and chuckled silently. Other evenings, they sat up on the rooftop, gazing up at the stars that sprinkled the deep blue sky, praying softly together. Mary watched Elizabeth's round stomach swell larger and larger, and all the while she delighted in the growing changes in her own body.

At last, after three months, Elizabeth decided that it was time Mary returned to Nazareth, before traveling became any more difficult for her. Mary was disappointed not to stay for the birth of Elizabeth's baby. He was due any day now, but she knew Elizabeth was right. Besides, it was time she once again faced her parents. . .and Joseph.

As they said good-bye, Elizabeth and Mary clung to each other and cried. "I will be praying for you," Elizabeth whispered. "Don't be afraid. God will work everything out."

Zechariah pressed Mary's hand silently. And then she squared her shoulders and turned toward the path that would lead her over the hills to Nazareth. By now, she thought as she walked, Joseph would surely have asked her father to release him from their betrothal. But God would be with her. . .no matter what.

The journey home passed quickly. She sang psalms as she walked, and at night she felt God's presence all around her as she slept. He was her companion wherever she went. Over and over, she hummed the words of her favorite psalm:

> *O Lord, you have examined my heart*
> *   and know everything about me.*
> *You know when I sit down or stand up.*
> *You know my every thought when far away.*
> *You chart the path ahead of me*
> *and tell me where to stop and rest.*
> *Every moment you know where I am.*
> *You know what I am going to say even before*
> *I say it, Lord.*
> *You both precede and follow me.*
> *You place your hand of blessing on my head.*
> *Such knowledge is too wonderful for me,*
> *   too great for me to know!*
> *I can never escape from your spirit!*
> *I can never get away from your presence!*
> *If I go up to heaven, you are there;*
> *If I go down to the place of the dead,*
> *   you are there.*

If I ride the wings of the morning,
*   if I dwell by the farthest oceans,*
*   even there your hand will guide me,*
*   and your strength will support me.*
You saw me before I was born.
Every day of my life was recorded in your book.
Every moment was laid out
*   before a single day had passed.*
How precious are your thoughts about me,
O God!
They are innumerable!
I can't even count them;
*   they outnumber the grains of sand!*
And when I wake up in the morning,
*   you are still with me!*
Search me, O God, and know my heart;
*   test me and know my thoughts.*
Point out anything in me that offends you,
*   and lead me along the path of everlasting life.*

As she sang, Mary was filled with a joy like she had never imagined was possible.

But as she drew closer to Nazareth, her feet moved slower. At last she stood on the hill above the village and looked down at the familiar houses. From here, their flat roofs and square clay walls made them look like a set of children's blocks scattered in the dusty valley. Mary drew in a deep breath and started down the hill. "I want Your will, Lord," she whispered. "Whatever it is. . ."

As she entered the narrow streets, her feet automatically started to take her to the small lane where Joseph's carpentry shop was. For the last couple of years, she had always snatched at any excuse to walk past his shop, hoping to catch a glimpse of him bent over his work or—better yet—exchange smiles and shy greetings with him. This time, though, she hesitated. Everything was different now.

Still, she had nothing of which to be ashamed. If he had decided to reject her, that was his right; she would grieve for him, but she would not hang her head. Not when the Son of God had already begun to flutter and kick inside her. "Yes," she said softly. "Whatever You want, Father."

She lifted her chin and started down the lane.

CHAPTER 4

Before she had taken more than a few steps, she found her shoulders grabbed from behind. She jumped and twirled around.

"It *is* you." Joseph stood looking down at her, breathing heavily as though he had been running. "You're home. I was just coming from your parents' when I thought I saw you up ahead. . . ." He drew in a deep breath while she stared at him with surprise; it almost sounded as though his voice was full of welcome. . .and something else that sounded like relief. She frowned, puzzled.

"I've missed you, Mary," he said softly, his hand still warm on her shoulder. "I was afraid you would never come home." And then he drew her closer, and his arms went tight around her. Mary let out a long trembly breath and pressed her face against his robe's rough fabric.

At last they stepped away from each other and smiled shyly. Mary searched his face. "You believe me now?"

He nodded. "Forgive me for not believing what you told me right from the beginning. But I. . ." He shrugged. His face clouded.

Mary touched his troubled mouth with her hand, delighted by her own daring. "It's all right," she said softly. "I understand. What changed your mind?"

He pressed his lips against her fingers, then took her

hand and began walking with her.

"I have to be honest with you," he said, and she heard the shame and regret in his voice. "I had decided to break our betrothal. I did not want you to be publicly disgraced, so I was going to do it quietly. But I was dreading talking to your father." He gave her a quick sideways glance. "And I hated to think I wasn't going to spend the rest of my life with you after all."

He touched a strand of her hair that had escaped her head covering. "One night as I was trying to think what I should do—and how I should do it—my thoughts kept circling round and round. I thought I would never fall asleep. I tried to pray, to put the end of our betrothal in God's hands, but I could find no peace.

"At last I must have fallen asleep. My dreams were broken, bits and pieces of nightmares. And then suddenly I realized that a. . .a being was standing next to my bed. The being was dressed in white, and he glowed so bright that my dark room was as light as noonday. At first I was frightened, but when I looked into the being's face, I saw he was smiling. . . ." His voice trailed away, as though he were still overwhelmed with wonder.

Mary nodded eagerly. "His name is Gabriel. That's what he told Zechariah."

Joseph stopped walking and turned to face her. "So your cousin's husband saw an angel, too? And you. . .and me. . ." His eyes met hers. "These are amazing times, Mary. To think that God is doing this. . .unbelievable thing in our life. Our child. . ." He fell silent, his eyes bright with awe.

"What did the angel say?" Mary prompted quietly.

Joseph drew in a deep sigh and began walking again. "I remember word by word—I've thought about it so many times while I waited for you to come home. He said, 'Joseph, son of David, do not be afraid to go ahead with your marriage to Mary. For the Child within her has been conceived by the Holy Spirit. And she will have a Son, and you are to name Him Jesus, for He will save His people from their sins.' "

Joseph stopped walking and faced Mary again, his face blazing with excitement. "Remember, Mary, what the prophet Isaiah said—'The virgin will conceive a child! She will give birth to a Son, and He will be called Immanuel.' "

Joseph's eyes dropped to Mary's stomach. "Think about what those names mean, Mary," he said softly. "Jesus means 'the Lord saves.' And Immanuel—'God is with us.' " His voice shook with wonder.

The Baby fluttered inside Mary's stomach, and she felt goose bumps run up her arms. "Yes," she whispered. "Yes."

Joseph looked into her eyes. "Will you marry me, Mary? Now? Tomorrow? As soon as we can?"

She smiled at the eagerness in his voice. "Yes," she said again.

Now that Joseph had also seen the angel, her parents believed her at last. With relief and joy and awe, they gave Mary to Joseph in marriage. Ema and Mary's sisters helped her pack her linens and other belongings, and Abba and her brothers carried them to Joseph's small house nearby. The days after her wedding were happy ones.

But just as she was settling down to wait for the birth of her Son, Joseph came home one afternoon from his carpenter's shop, his face troubled.

"What is it?" Mary asked him after he had washed his hands and said a prayer of thanksgiving for their supper. "What's worrying you?"

Joseph took a swallow of the lentil soup Mary had made. Then he sighed. "It's that emperor in Rome. He's decided he wants a census taken of the entire nation. Everyone has to go to the city of their ancestors." He met Mary's eyes. "I'm sorry. I hate to have you traveling now. We're going to have to go to Bethlehem."

This wasn't what Mary had expected. As she looked around Bethlehem's busy streets, her heart longed for home. She missed quiet Nazareth; she missed her mother's gentle hands and her father's smile. She had imagined her baby being born at home, where she would have felt safe and loved. Not here in this strange, bustling place, full of the noise of animals and the frustrated voices of too many people in too small a space.

Joseph hadn't even been able to find them a room in the inn. Mary sighed and leaned over their donkey's back as Joseph led it to the stable behind the inn. At least she could get down soon, and then surely there would be somewhere she could lie down. . . .

Once she was stretched out on Joseph's cloak on top of a pile of straw, she fell asleep almost immediately. She didn't sleep long, though. When she opened her eyes, she looked around the stable. Their donkey was eating hay next to a tired-looking cow, and two sleepy chickens roosted on the rafter above her head. A sheep lay in the straw beside Mary, its legs tucked neatly beneath it while it thoughtfully chewed its cud.

Mary pushed herself up and rubbed her back, then settled back against the manger. The air was filled with the smell of animals, but at least it was quiet and peaceful here. *Yes, Lord,* she prayed. *Even here, even now. If this is where You want Your Son to be born, then I will still say yes.*

Joseph came through the stable door, carrying the supper he had bought them at the inn. His eyes were worried as he looked down at Mary. "How are you? Can you eat anything?"

She shook her head. Joseph knelt beside her, his hands on her shoulders. He met her eyes. "How soon do you think it will be until. . . ?"

Mary took a shaky breath and smiled. "Soon."

Later that night, tears of joy streaked her face as she looked down at her newborn son. She touched His tiny, squirming feet and ran a finger along His petal-soft cheek. Then carefully, as she had seen Ema do with her younger brothers and sisters, she wrapped Him tight and warm in clean swaddling cloths. Exhausted, she drifted off to sleep, holding in her arms God in a tiny human body.

An hour or two later, Joseph shook her gently awake. "We have visitors," he told her softly.

Mary reached for the baby, but her lap was empty. Joseph must have laid Him in the manger; He was still sleeping soundly, undisturbed. She looked up and found the stable door crowded with strange men. She wiped the sleep from her eyes and sat up. They were shepherds, she realized, for some of them still clutched their shepherds' crooks in their gnarled hands. Their eyes were wide with wonder.

"We were w–w–watching our sheep," one of them stuttered, "w–when all of a sudden a strange man was there w–with us on the hill. We—"

"He shone so bright that it might as well have been

midday," another interrupted. "We were scared, but—"

"He told us not to be afraid," the first one finished.

A younger man stepped into the doorway. He was barely more than a boy, Mary saw, and his bright gaze was fastened on the baby where He lay in the manger. "The angel said to us, 'Don't be afraid! I bring you good news of great joy for everyone! The Savior—yes, the Messiah, the Lord—has been born tonight in Bethlehem, the city of David!' " The boy's eyes were dreamy as he quoted the angel's words. "He told us that we would recognize the baby because He would be like this—" He waved a hand at the baby. "Lying in a manger, wrapped tight in strips of cloth." The boy's eyes were full of stars as he turned back to Mary. "And then suddenly the angel was joined by more angels, hundreds and hundreds of them filling up the sky. They were singing."

"Did you understand their song?" Mary asked softly, curious to know more about these heavenly creatures.

The shepherd boy nodded. "They sang, 'Glory to God in the highest heaven, and peace on earth, goodwill among people.' " He sighed and fell silent.

"And then we left our sheep and ran all the way here," the first shepherd said. He added gruffly, "We wanted to see for ourselves."

Mary smiled at the shepherds, and then she leaned over the manger. Gently, she unwrapped the baby a little so they could see His face. Joseph motioned for the shepherds to come into the stable, and they filed in, then stood in a cluster looking down at the baby. He squirmed, then opened His eyes and looked gravely up toward the shepherds' hovering faces. After a moment, one by one, the shepherds went down on their knees.

When they had gone, Mary leaned against Joseph's shoulder, thinking over everything that had happened. The baby slept peacefully in Joseph's arms now, and even the cow and the sheep had fallen asleep. The whole world was hushed and quiet. *If my heart is Your mansion, Lord,* Mary thought sleepily, *then how full the rooms are getting with treasures.*

She let her eyes fall shut, glad that she had dared to say yes to God. As she drifted off to sleep, her last thought was, *What wonderful thing will You do next, God?*

CHAPTER 6

Eight days later, Mary and Joseph took the baby to be circumcised in the synagogue. At the ceremony, they gave Him the name the angel had told Joseph to use: Jesus. It was a common name in Galilee; no one raised an eyebrow when they told the rabbi the name they had chosen for their son.

But Mary and Joseph looked at each other and smiled. They knew that their baby's name had not been chosen by them. It had been given to them by the angel Gabriel, and its meaning would be fulfilled by their child's life. *The Lord saves.* Mary said the words to herself as she held Jesus in her arms. Every time she said her child's name, she realized, she would be affirming her faith in God. The Lord saves!

A month or so later, the time came for Mary and Joseph to go to the temple in Jerusalem. Jewish law said that on the fortieth day after a son's birth, the mother must go to the temple to be purified. The Torah also said, "If a woman's first child is a boy, he must be dedicated to the Lord." So Mary carefully packed their clothes for the short trip, tucking plenty of diapers for Jesus into their bags.

When they reached Jerusalem, they made their way through the busy streets to the temple. Joseph carried a cage with two pigeons for a sacrifice to God. Mary carried Jesus in her arms. She held Him carefully, fearful that the crowd might jostle Him out of her arms, her cheek pressed against His soft head.

As soon as she had said yes to the angel's message, she had begun to love Him, and she had learned to love Him more during the months when she had carried Him inside her body. But now that He was here, where she could hold Him in her arms, look into His eyes, and touch His tiny hands, she loved Him in a new and different way. He was hers. . . her baby. Her heart nearly broke every time she thought of danger threatening Him. She would do anything to keep Him safe.

As they neared the temple, Mary looked up at the tall columns, and she held Jesus even tighter. For some reason, she was dreading today's ceremony. Something inside her didn't want to give Jesus to God. He was hers. She sighed and followed Joseph through the bronze gate that led into the women's court of the temple.

Before they could go very far, an old man came up to them, his face bright with welcome and joy. He almost seemed to have been waiting for them, Mary thought, and yet she was certain she had never seen him before.

"My name is Simeon," he said, and his old voice quavered with emotion, as though he might cry. His eyes were fixed on the bundle in Mary's arms. "May I see your child?"

Mary hesitated, but something in the man's old, wrinkled face reassured her. She unwrapped Jesus' covering and turned Him so that the old man could see His face.

Simeon let out a long sigh. "At last," he breathed. "At last." He shut his eyes, and his lips moved silently in prayer.

After a moment, he smiled and opened his eyes. "I have been waiting for this moment for a long, long time."

Joseph was studying the old man's face thoughtfully. "What do you mean?" he asked.

Simeon turned to Joseph. "I am an old man." His smile grew wider. "As you can no doubt see. Over the years, I have watched our nation fall deeper and deeper under Rome's control, and I have grieved for Israel. I am all alone, for my wife and my sons and daughters have all died. Year after year, I grew more and more lonely—but still I continued to pray to God to rescue our nation. I believed that the Messiah would come, just as the prophets said He would. But year after year, nothing changed. I saw no sign of the Messiah. And I grew lonelier and lonelier.

"Some years ago, I told God that I was ready to die and be with Him. But I felt God's Spirit tell me, 'No. This is not your time.' After that I was filled with a strange restlessness. I continued to pray—and one day I felt the Spirit say to me, as clear as I hear you, 'You will not die until you see the Lord's Messiah.' "

Simeon turned away from Joseph, back to Jesus, his faded eyes bright with tears. "This morning I was enjoying the sunshine in my garden, when I felt the Spirit nudge me. 'Get up,' He said to me. 'Go to the temple.' " Simeon shrugged. "At first I told myself it was my imagination. But then the Spirit's call was too clear to be mistaken. And so I came. . . and as I walked through the gate, I saw the baby."

His lined face was soft with love. "Could I hold Him, do

you think?" He turned toward Mary, his voice humble. "Just for a moment?"

Mary smiled and held Jesus out to him. Simeon took the baby in his arms, and for a long moment he looked down into Jesus' face. The baby looked back at him soberly, then reached out and tangled His small fist in Simeon's long, white beard. Simeon smiled.

"Lord," he said softly, his voice full of adoration and awe, "now I can die in peace! As You promised me, I have seen the Savior You have given to all people. He is a light to reveal God to the nations, and He is the glory of Your people Israel!"

Joseph and Mary exchanged looks of surprise. They knew their son was special; they had not forgotten all the angels who had been involved with His coming. And yet now that He was here and they were so busy caring for Him, feeding Him, and changing His diapers, sometimes they forgot that He was not only their baby, but the Savior.

Simeon looked into Mary's face. "This baby belongs to all of us," he said gently, and she heard the understanding in his voice. "God sent Him for us all."

He put the baby back in her arms, and then he raised his hands and blessed both her and Joseph. When he had finished praying, he again turned to Mary. His eyes met hers for a long moment.

"This child will be rejected by many in Israel," he said, "and it will be their undoing. But He will be the greatest joy to many others. The deepest thoughts of many hearts will be revealed." Simeon's face was grave, and he reached out and touched Mary's hand where it clasped Jesus. "And a sword will pierce your very soul, Daughter."

Mary felt a shiver run across her skin. "What do you—?" she started to ask, but before she could finish her question, an old woman rushed up to her, her wrinkled face glowing with joy.

"Praise God!" the woman cried. She looked at Jesus, and tears of joy ran down her lined cheeks. "Praise God! He is here at last!"

Simeon nodded. "Yes, Anna, He is here at last."

The two old people spent a long time with Mary and Joseph and the baby. They put their gnarled fingers in His tiny hands, they smiled down into His face, they took turns holding Him close against their hearts. Mary smiled as she watched them, but inside her heart, she was hearing again Simeon's words: *A sword will pierce your very soul.*

But Jesus' birth had brought her nothing but joy. How could anything about Him ever send a sword into her soul?

As they said good-bye to Simeon and Anna, she pushed the thought away. Surely, Simeon was wrong. He was so old after all.

As they crossed the temple courtyard to give their pigeons to the priest, she looked back over her shoulder at Simeon and Anna. Anna was praising God again, her cracked old voice loud with triumph. Everyone who passed by her she grabbed and cried, "Have you heard what has happened?" Mary could hear her from all the way across the courtyard. But Simeon was still standing where they had left him, watching them.

Across the courtyard, his eyes met Mary's.

The compassion in his gaze made her hold Jesus tighter. *He knows what lies ahead,* she realized. *God's Spirit has told him.* She looked down at Jesus' small, downy head, and her eyes burned with tears.

But the time had come now for them to give Jesus to God. Mary turned Jesus around in her arms, but before she handed Him to the priest, she hesitated for a long moment. She looked down into her Son's face. *How can I bear it if something should ever happen to Him?*

Joseph touched her arm. "Mary?"

She sighed. A tear rolled down her cheek. *Yes, Lord,* her heart whispered. *Even then, if You should allow something to happen to this precious One. . .even then, I still say yes. He is Yours. You gave Him to me. Now I give Him back to You.* She put her baby in the priest's arms to be dedicated to God.

Mary and Joseph took the baby back to the house they had rented in Bethlehem. Joseph had opened a small carpentry shop to support them, and Mary was busy caring for the baby. Each day He seemed to grow bigger, and they were delighted by all the new things He was learning to do. He could sit up; then He could crawl; then He could pull Himself up on His tottery, plump legs.

"E-ma!" He called early one morning, waking them from their sleep, and together they celebrated His first word. The next week He learned to say Abba, and then He was stringing whole chains of words together, babbling at Mary while she ground their grain, playing at Joseph's feet with scraps of wood, chuckling to Himself. Each day, they loved Him more.

And then one evening, when Jesus was nearly two years old, three strangers came to their door.

CHAPTER 7

"We have company, Mary," Joseph said as he came in from his shop.

He hadn't had a chance to wash yet, she saw when she looked up from her sewing, for he had sawdust clinging to his beard and hair. She smiled and looked past him, expecting to see one of the neighbors from down the street. Instead, a man in a long silk robe stood in the doorway. Startled, Mary put down her sewing and got to her feet.

The man's eyes were different than any she had ever seen, and his skin was another shade of tan than their own. He held his head proudly, but his eyes were full of curiosity and wonder.

"Come in," Joseph said to him and motioned him deeper into their house. The man's long robe whispered on the dirt floor as he came toward Mary—and behind him followed two more men, each dressed as richly as he. Their narrow faces were full of wisdom and pride.

Jesus had been playing quietly in the corner with the wooden blocks Joseph had made Him, but now He toddled forward to investigate these newcomers. When they saw Him, the three men's faces changed. Mary was suddenly reminded of the way the shepherds' faces had looked on the night when Jesus was born—awed and humbled and joyful, all at the same time. *They know,* she realized. *These men know Who my son is.*

Amazed, she watched as the three proud men in their rich robes went down on their knees on her dirt floor. They bowed their heads before her little son. Mary turned toward Jesus, wondering what He would do. He stood still for a moment, looking gravely at the three men—and then He smiled and came forward. One by one, He gently put His small hands on their faces. Mary and Joseph watched while tears leaked out of the men's eyes and ran down their proud cheeks.

"We are royal astrologers," one of the three men explained over dinner. "We come from a land far to the East. Almost two years ago, we saw a new star in the East, and we knew that the time had come for the King of the Jews to be born. We wanted to worship Him, and so we followed the star." He paused and looked across the table at Jesus. "The star brought us here."

"But we stopped first to ask directions from Herod," one of the others reminded.

"Herod?" Joseph frowned.

"We went to Jerusalem first," explained the third man. "We were expecting to find the new king among the royal court." His eyes traveled around the small room, and then his gaze settled on Jesus' face. "We should have known better," he murmured.

"What did Herod have to say?" Joseph asked uneasily. He didn't trust Herod, Mary knew, especially not since they had heard of the murders in Herod's own house. Herod had killed his own family to ensure his rule—and meanwhile he strictly followed the Torah's diet, never eating any pork or other meat that the Law did not allow. "As though that will do him any good when he stands before God," Joseph would mutter. "The hypocrite. I'd rather be Herod's pig than Herod's son."

Thinking of Herod made Mary shiver. She wanted to scoop Jesus up on her lap and hold Him tight, but He was eating happily, sharing bites of food with the astrologer beside Him.

"What did Herod say?" Joseph repeated.

The three men exchanged glances. "He was upset," one of them admitted. "Obviously, he knew of no ruler but himself—and he wasn't happy about the idea. He called a meeting of all the priests and rabbis, and he asked them where your prophets had predicted that the Messiah would be born. They were the ones who first directed us toward Bethlehem."

Another of the men stroked his long black beard thoughtfully. "After that, Herod sent for us privately. He spent a long time asking us questions about the star we had seen."

"What sort of questions?" Joseph asked, his voice tense.

"He wanted to know exactly when we had first seen the star."

Mary looked from Joseph's worried face to Jesus' unconcerned one. *Herod knows about our son now,* she realized. *And he knows about how old He is.* Fear clutched at her, but then Jesus smiled at His mother. Her heart lightened, and she smiled back at Him before turning once more to the three astrologers. "Did Herod say anything else?" she asked.

Again the three men glanced at each other. "He told us to go to Bethlehem and search carefully for the child," one of them said.

" 'And when you find Him,' " one of the other astrologers mimicked Herod's gruff voice, " 'come back and tell me so that I can go and worship Him, too!' "

Across the table, Mary and Joseph met each other's eyes.

When they had finished eating, the astrologers brought in their packs from their camels. They opened them and brought out treasure chests full of gold and frankincense. "These are for the child," one of them said.

Jesus explored the costly gifts with His small chubby hands, delighted by the bright colors of the jewels that studded the chests. When He found a brilliant blue and scarlet feather tucked in among the gold, He was more pleased with that than with anything else. Even Joseph, who had barely spoken since supper, laughed as he watched Him play.

Amid the commotion, Mary watched her husband's face. He was uncomfortable and awed by the riches spilled out across his floor, she knew, but the tension in his face was caused by something more than embarrassment. He was worried about Herod.

One of the astrologers placed yet another gift at Jesus' feet. "My gift," he said quietly. "Myrrh."

Mary shivered, and her eyes sought Joseph's. He gave a little shrug of his shoulders, as though he were advising her not to make too much of the astrologer's strange gift. After all, perhaps in their country they did not use myrrh as a spice for burial. Still, it seemed like an odd gift for a baby. She reached for Jesus and held Him close. His little body was warm and wiggly against her, and she refused to think that anyone would ever wrap His dead body with white linen and myrrh. Surely, God would keep His Son safe from death. He of all people would never have to face death's cold darkness.

The three astrologers spent the night outside the house, sleeping on the ground with their camels, and in the morning they came inside again to eat with Mary and Joseph and Jesus. Mary was tired, for her sleep had been broken, but she tried to smile as she handed out the food bowls. "Did you sleep well?"

"No," the oldest one said. "We did not." He looked at the others, as though he wondered what more he should say.

"Our sleep was troubled by dreams," another of them said.

The one whose skin was darker than the others met Mary's eyes. "We will be on our way this morning, back to our own land. But we will not go through Jerusalem this time. We will not return to Herod as he requested."

Mary heard Joseph let out a long breath. "Why not?" he asked gruffly.

The dark-skinned astrologer turned toward him. "God spoke to me," he said simply. "In a dream. He told me not to tell Herod what we found here." His eyes went to Jesus. Jesus looked back at him and smiled. "We will not tell him," the man said softly.

The astrologers spent the morning with Jesus, quietly watching Him play and listening to His voice, and then they went on their way. After they were gone, Joseph went back to his shop. He had said very little all morning, and Mary could see the lines of tension that creased his forehead. She held Jesus on her lap for a long time, rocking Him and singing to Him, her heart full of fears for the future.

"Mary! Wake up, Mary!"

In the middle of the night, Joseph's voice made her jump up from her sleep, her heart pounding. She stared around the dark house. "What is it?"

"I had a dream." Joseph's voice was soft and urgent. "I saw the angel again. We have to leave."

"Now?" Mary's heart was heavy with dread. She scrambled across their sleeping mat and touched Jesus' tousled curls where He lay sleeping quietly beside them. "What did —what did the angel say?" she whispered.

Joseph took a deep breath. "He said, 'Get up and flee to Egypt with the child and His mother. Stay there until I tell you to return, because Herod is going to try to kill the child.' "

Mary sank back on their mat, her hand still resting on Jesus' head. "Can we wait until morning?" She hated to wake Jesus. She hated to set out with Him in the darkness for a strange land where she had never been. "Why Egypt?"

Joseph had already lit a lamp and was starting to pack their belongings. "Come on, Mary," he said over his shoulder. "We may not have much time. Herod may already be sending his soldiers to search out all the baby boys."

Mary hesitated a moment longer. They were settled here

in Bethlehem now. They had been so happy these last two years. She closed her eyes tightly. "Yes, Lord," she whispered at last. "I will accept whatever You want."

She got to her feet and began to pack for the long journey to Egypt.

Almost a year later, Mary lay watching the morning sun shine through the window of their small Egyptian house. Jesus was also awake, but although He turned His head now and then to smile at His mother, He, too, was silent, lying quietly as He watched the sunlight filter through the palm fronds beyond the window.

Beside her, Joseph was still asleep. All night, he had tossed and turned, muttering in his sleep, and Mary hated to wake him, though she knew he would need to leave soon for his carpentry shop. She should get up and stir the fire to life, dress herself and Jesus, and prepare their morning meal. And after that, she should go to the market to buy food for their supper.

She sighed. Life seemed so much more complicated here in Egypt where everyone spoke a different language, where her family and friends were so far away. A simple thing like going to the market wore her out. For just a moment longer, she decided, she would simply lie here, enjoying the morning quiet, close to the two people she loved most in all the world.

"Would you like to start home today?" asked Joseph's quiet voice.

Her heart leaped. She turned her head and saw that Joseph's eyes were open.

He nodded, answering the unspoken question in her eyes. "I saw the angel again last night. He said, 'Get up and take the child and His mother back to the land of Israel, because those who were trying to kill the child are dead.' " Joseph ran his thumb gently along Mary's cheek. "We can go home now, Mary. He'll be safe."

Tears of joy stung Mary's eyes. She closed her eyes and whispered a prayer of praise to God.

The trip home was a happy one, not like the rushed and fearful journey the year before when they had fled from Herod. This time they laughed and talked and enjoyed the scenery. Jesus was old enough that they could point things out to Him, and He looked at everything with interest and delight.

As they traveled closer to Bethlehem, the hills began to look familiar, and Mary grew excited at the thought of being back with her friends. They reached Judea late one afternoon, and Mary told Jesus, "Maybe we'll sleep tonight in Bethlehem, where You were born."

They stopped to rest for a moment beside the road. While Mary gave Jesus a drink and a bite of bread, Joseph heard the noise of travelers coming toward them. "Let me go hear what news they have of Bethlehem," he said and walked down the road to meet them.

He stood talking with the travelers for a long time before they went on their way. When he turned back toward her, Mary's heart sank at the stern look on his face. "I don't like it," he said to her when he had rejoined his family. "Herod's will left Judea to his son Archelaus. They say he hates the Jews even more than his father did. He has already put to death hundreds of our people."

Mary reached for Jesus' small hand and clutched it tightly. He looked up at her, His little face full of love and peace, and she smiled down at Him. "It will be all right," she told Joseph. "The angel would not have told you to come home if we would not be safe."

Joseph nodded, but his eyes were still clouded with worry. "We will spend the night here," he said at last, "instead of pressing on for Bethlehem. I will pray about this. I want to be sure we are doing what God wants."

Mary nodded. "I will pray, too." She thought of Gabriel, the angel who had spoken to her nearly four years before. Although she had never seen him again, she believed he was the same angel who spoke to Joseph in his dreams. She liked to think of him walking with them each day, invisible to their eyes, his bright face turned always toward her Son, making sure no harm befell Him. Heaven was watching over Jesus, she had no doubt, and she smiled at Joseph, trying to reassure him. "God will take care of us," she told him as they began to make camp for the night. "We don't need to be afraid."

When Mary awoke the next morning, Joseph was already up, getting their donkey ready for the day's journey. Jesus was helping him, chattering to His father all the while. Mary smiled and stretched, then got up and prepared their morning meal.

Once they had eaten, they lifted Jesus on the donkey and began to walk. Joseph was not leading them toward Bethlehem, though, Mary realized. She looked up at him, surprised. "Where are we going?"

"What would you think about going home?"

"But Bethlehem is that way." She pointed with her finger.

"I know." He smiled. "I meant Nazareth."

"Nazareth?" Her face lit up with joy. To be close to Ema and Abba again and her brothers and sisters. . .home.

Joseph nodded. "Nazareth is in Galilee. Herod's son Antipas rules there now, not Archelaus."

"And we'll be safe there?" Mary searched Joseph's face, looking for the fear she had read there yesterday.

"Yes." Joseph's face was calm and certain now. "We'll be safe in Nazareth. We can settle down at last."

Mary gave a skip of happiness. Then she glanced up again at Joseph. "You seem very sure about this. Have you been talking with a certain angel lately?"

He grinned. And she knew from the look of joy and peace in his eyes that Gabriel had visited her husband once again.

Her family was delighted to have them back in Nazareth, and they settled quickly into their old routines. Joseph went each day to his old carpentry shop, the same one where he had worked when Mary first met him, and Mary busied herself each day with caring for her family. As Jesus grew older, He delighted them more and more. Everyone who knew Him loved Him. Even those who knew nothing of the wonder and mystery of His birth could tell that there was something unusual about Him, something joyful and loving that drew people to Him.

As Mary watched Jesus grow, she never forgot all the strange things that had happened during His early years, but she was glad that life was calmer now. As the years went by, each one so much like the one before, she wondered sometimes what God had in store for her son. Just as quickly, she put the thought out of her mind. Wasn't it enough that Jesus was happy and healthy and safe? Would God ask anything more? With a little flicker of fear, she realized she almost wished that her child was like any other child, with no enormous destiny waiting in His future.

When Jesus was twelve years old, Mary and Joseph took Him to Jerusalem for the Passover festival, just as they had every year since they had returned to Nazareth. As always, Mary enjoyed the chance to be with friends and family who lived outside of Nazareth. She and Elizabeth were particularly glad to see one another, for they had remained close down through the years, even though they'd had few chances to be together. No other woman understood Mary's heart as much as Elizabeth did, and each year she looked forward to the chance to sit and talk with her.

When the festival was over, the band of travelers from Nazareth started home. Mary rode their donkey, enjoying the chance to talk with her mother and sisters as they traveled. She could see Joseph ahead of them, talking with the other men, and she assumed that Jesus was with the troop of children that ran along beside them, laughing and playing games as they went.

When they stopped for their evening meal, the crowd of

people setting up camp was so thick that Mary could not see either her son or her husband. She began to help prepare the supper, knowing that her family was bound to turn up soon, and she was not surprised when she felt Joseph's hand on her waist.

"There you are." He smiled down at her. "I knew if I found the cooking fire, I'd be bound to find you, too. Where's Jesus?"

Mary skewered some fresh meat and bent to lay the stick across the embers. "He must be with His friends somewhere. I haven't seen Him since this morning."

She stood up straight and searched the crowd of people milling around, feeling her first flicker of uneasiness. Jesus was more independent now that He was older, but she was very close to her son, and He usually talked to her often throughout the day.

Joseph wiped a smudge of charcoal off her cheek and smiled. "Don't worry. I'll find Him. There's a group of kids playing some sort of game up on the hill. He's probably with them."

But He wasn't. And He wasn't with His grandfather or His uncles. He wasn't with any of their friends. Mary and Joseph had asked everyone if they had seen Him; no one had. At last, her stomach sick with fear, Mary met Joseph's eyes. "Where can He be?" she cried.

Joseph was already packing up their donkey. "Come on," he said. "We'll go back to Jerusalem. Somehow He must have been left behind."

Three days later, they finally found Him. He was in the temple, sitting in the middle of a group of rabbis, deep in conversation. A small crowd had gathered around them to listen. Jesus didn't even look up when His parents joined the circle of people.

Mary's heart pounded with relief as she looked at her son. He was safe after all. The last three days had been a nightmare as they searched everywhere they had been during the festival. They had never thought till now to look in the temple. After all, what would a child do in the temple?

What was He doing here? Mary edged closer through the people. "Please, let me through," she said desperately, anxious to touch Jesus, longing to know for sure He was really safe. Where had He been sleeping these last three nights? What had He eaten?

"Shh!" the person next to her said. "I want to hear the boy's answer to that last question."

Mary tried to listen, too, but she was too upset to understand her son's words. She saw only that He looked happy and calm; He had obviously not been missing His mother and father.

After a moment, the man beside her turned to her. "Can you believe that a youngster like that would have such wisdom?" He shook his head. "How could a boy know such things? They say His name is Jesus of Nazareth."

"Yes," Mary said impatiently. "I know. He's my son." At last she managed to push through the crowd, and she grabbed Jesus by the arm.

"What were You thinking of?" she asked Him, her voice shrill with fear and relief. "Why would You scare us like this? Your father and I have been frantic, searching for You everywhere."

He looked up at her, surprised. "But why did you need to search?" He asked her. "You should have known that I would be in My Father's house."

"What are You talking about? Your father's house? Your father's house is back in Nazareth—which is where You would be right now if You had been where You were supposed to be."

Jesus didn't answer; He only looked into His mother's eyes. Mary drew in a deep breath. *He knows,* she realized. *He knows Who He is.*

Their journey home to Nazareth was a quiet one. Joseph had started to scold Jesus for worrying them, and then he had fallen silent. Over Jesus' head, Mary and Joseph exchanged looks, their expressions confused and troubled.

Their life had been ordinary and quiet for so many years that they had both stopped thinking much about the angel who had guided them so often years before. But now Mary thought of him again. She wondered if Gabriel had been seated in the temple, listening to her son, learning from His words along with the rabbis and the rest.

She would like to sit down with Gabriel and have a talk some day, she thought. Maybe he could explain to her what her son's purpose on earth was to be. She smiled, picturing Gabriel and herself having a chat some afternoon, the way she and Ema so often did, and she tried to imagine what he would say to her.

He is not only your son, Mary. He is God's Son, too.

She did not hear the words out loud, and she saw no vision as Joseph had those four times. But she was suddenly certain that these were the words the angel would say to her.

Mary shivered. She put her hand on their donkey's warm neck, and she watched Jesus as He walked beside Joseph. *He is still just a child,* she comforted herself. *What could God want with Him now?*

As though He sensed her gaze, Jesus turned and smiled at her, His gaze as bright and loving as always. *He is God's Son, too.* The words echoed in her mind.

Mary took a deep breath, and then she lifted her head and squared her shoulders. *Yes, Lord. I want whatever You say.*

As the years went by, Mary said yes to God again and again as she watched Jesus grow taller and wiser with each passing month. He never again frightened them the way He had the year He was twelve. He seemed to understand that He needed to balance His responsibility to them, His earthly parents, with His responsibility to His heavenly Father.

When He reached adulthood and still their lives continued

as quiet and uneventful as ever, Joseph wondered out loud to Mary if this quiet, simple life was all that God had planned for their son.

"After all," he said, "maybe this is enough. He is an excellent carpenter. He is kind and loving to everyone. That way He has of listening so carefully to each person who talks to Him—it comforts people somehow. Maybe that is what the Lord is saying to us—that a quiet, honest, loving life is as pleasing to Him as fame and power."

"Yes," Mary said, her brow wrinkled. She knew that through her son she had a new vision of the God she had served all her life. Before, God had always seemed distant somehow, a powerful, loving image that she could only catch glimpses of far in the distance. But now, God lived with her. He smiled at her every morning and touched her face with His familiar hand, He laughed at her table and thanked her for her smallest service to Him, and His arms were strong and warm when she was sad or afraid.

And yet at the same time, He was her son, and she would give her life to keep Him safe and whole and happy. She sighed, her heart shadowed with fear. Although she said nothing to Joseph, somehow she was sure that God had something more in store for Jesus, something beyond the quiet, simple life He had lived with them so far.

When Jesus was thirty years old, the family traveled to Bethany, where Mary's cousin Elizabeth now lived. Zechariah had died a few years earlier, and Elizabeth had grown very feeble, but she and Mary still loved to sit and talk just as they always had. Mary was looking forward to that part of their visit, but for some reason she was dreading seeing Elizabeth's son John again.

John had grown into a strange young man. All his life he had been blunt and outspoken, but now he had a wildness about him that made Mary uncomfortable. He practiced no trade, and he no longer lived with his mother. Instead, he spent most of his time alone in the wilderness, wandering around dressed in a rough camel-hair robe that he bound with a leather belt. Elizabeth had told her that he ate only what he could find from the land, mostly locusts and wild honey. The very thought had made Mary cringe, but Elizabeth seemed unconcerned by her son's odd behavior. Mary, however, was glad that her own son lived such an ordinary, quiet life.

Recently, Mary and Joseph had heard that people had begun to seek John out in the wilderness, so that they could listen to him speak and be baptized by him in the Jordan River. He was said to be a fiery preacher, speaking out against corruption, both in the government and in people's hearts, and rumors were traveling around the country that John might even be the Messiah, the Anointed One who would rescue Israel from its bondage to Rome.

Joseph was eager to hear John preach, but Jesus had not commented on His cousin's ministry. Mary knew that He had heard the gossip, but He said nothing. He continued to help Joseph in the carpentry shop, just as He always had, and yet somehow the rumors about John made Mary uneasy. Something was changing, she sensed, and on the journey to Bethany she stayed close to Jesus, comforted by the peace she always felt in His presence.

As they neared Bethany, they noticed a large crowd gathered along the Jordan River, and they heard a man's voice shouting. Joseph lifted his head. "That's John! Let's go hear him."

Mary hung back. "Can't we go to Elizabeth's house first? She's expecting us, and I am tired."

Jesus took His mother's hand. "Come, Ema," He said quietly.

She looked up at Him and met His gaze. As always, she saw the love and gentleness in His eyes, but she also saw a glimpse of the same strength and resolution she had first seen in Him in the temple when He was twelve. He smiled. "Will you come, Ema?"

She sighed. "Yes. I will come with You."

As they drew nearer, she caught sight of John's wild curls rising above the heads of the crowd, and she knew he must be standing on something, a great stone maybe, or an up-turned boat beside the riverbank. His dark eyes flashed, and his words made her shiver.

"You brood of snakes!" he shouted. "Prove by the way you live that you have really turned from your sins and turned to God. Don't just say, 'We're safe—we're the descendants of Abraham.' That proves nothing. God can change these stones here into children of Abraham."

He waved his hand, and as the crowd parted a little, Mary saw that he was standing on a heap of tumbled river stone. Mary looked at the round, gray stones, and she thought suddenly of another stone, a small round pebble that had dropped straight through Gabriel's hand.

She shivered again, but this time with a sense of joy and awe. God could do anything, and as she looked at John's wild, strong face, she knew he was not speaking poetically: John believed without a doubt in his mind that if God wanted, He could turn those ordinary stones into people, His people.

Lately, when Mary thought of God's great mansion, she imagined herself living in some small, quiet room, filled with sunlight and the ordinary smell of bread baking. She did not like to picture all the other strange rooms in the Lord's huge dwelling-place. Instead, she was content with the safe little corner He had given her, and she prayed that He would let her live out her days there, worshiping Him peacefully and quietly.

But now, something in John's words made her remember how great her Lord was and how immense was His mansion. She sensed in John a burning joy, and she knew he would stride fearlessly from room to room of God's home, wherever the Lord's Spirit led him. *Help me to have courage, Lord,* Mary whispered in her heart. *Help me to say yes to wherever You lead me.*

As though He had read her thoughts, Jesus stepped closer to her and brushed a kiss against her forehead. She looked up at Him, but He only smiled and turned back to listen to His cousin.

"Even now," John was saying, "the ax of God's judgment is poised, ready to sever your roots. Yes, every tree that does not produce good fruit will be chopped down and thrown into the fire."

Someone in the crowd shouted out to him, "What should we do?"

John turned toward the voice, his eyes glowing. "If you have two coats, give one to the poor. If you have food, share it with those who are hungry."

"How simple," Joseph said to Mary, "and yet how different our world would be if we all followed his direction."

There was a stir in the crowd, and a group of men pressed forward toward John. Joseph bent his head and whispered in Mary's ear, "Do you recognize those men? They're priests and Levites from the temple in Jerusalem." He looked grim. "I'm afraid John may find himself in trouble one of these days."

"Do you claim to be the Messiah?" one of the men asked John.

John turned to look at the man, his expression unreadable. "I am not the Messiah," he said flatly.

"Well then, who are you?" someone in the crowd shouted. "Are you Elijah?"

"No," John answered.

"Are you the Prophet?"

John grinned. "No, I am not."

"Then who are you?" asked one of the men from the temple. "Tell us, so we can give an answer to those who sent us. What do you have to say about yourself?"

John hesitated, his face thoughtful, and then he lifted his head and said clearly, "I am a voice shouting in the wilderness, 'Prepare a straight pathway for the Lord's coming!' "

Mary recognized his words as ones that the prophet Isaiah had spoken hundreds of years earlier, and the certainty and strength in John's voice made goose bumps creep across her skin. She looked up at Jesus, looking for some sort of reassurance, but His eyes were on His cousin. His face was as calm as ever, but she sensed that He was waiting for something.

"If you aren't the Messiah or Elijah or the Prophet," said one of the men from the temple, "what right do you have to baptize people the way you do?"

John shrugged his wide shoulders. "I baptize with water, but right here in the crowd is Someone you do not know, who will soon begin His ministry. I am not even worthy to be His slave." He looked over the heads of the people, directly at his cousin Jesus. "I baptize you with water, but He will baptize you with the Holy Spirit."

That night they sat late around Elizabeth's table, talking about the amazing way John spoke to people's hearts. Mary saw that Elizabeth was proud of her son, but Mary couldn't keep herself from asking her cousin as they cleared away the dishes, "Don't you worry what will happen to him? The Pharisees and the other temple officials will not be happy with what he is saying. They will be bound to make trouble for him."

Elizabeth only smiled. "He must follow his calling. I knew that from the moment he was conceived." Her faded eyes went to Jesus where He sat beside the fire with Joseph. "My son is like the person who lays a foundation," Elizabeth said softly. "It is your son who will build the house."

Mary looked at Jesus for a long moment, and then she drew in a deep breath. She went to Him and knelt beside Him on the floor, looking up into His face. "Is it true then?" she asked softly. "Are You about to begin something new? Some ministry that will show others Who You are?"

He smiled at her. "I must do what God tells me."

"What will You do?" Joseph asked Him quietly.

Jesus looked at His two earthly parents, His love for them clear in His gaze. He shrugged. "Well, to start with, I will ask John to baptize Me."

CHAPTER 10

Mary was not there to see when her son was baptized, but she heard the story later from Elizabeth, who had heard it from her son.

At first, John had been reluctant to do what his cousin asked. "I am the one who needs to be baptized by You," he said, "so why are You coming to me?"

But Jesus answered him, "It must be done, because we must do everything that is right." So then John baptized Him.

"Afterward," Elizabeth told Mary, "as Jesus came up out of the water, an amazing thing happened. John says it looked as though a door opened into heaven—and a dove fluttered out and flew straight to Jesus. It settled on His shoulder, and John heard a voice speak from heaven. The voice said, 'You are My beloved Son, and I am fully pleased with You.'"

As Mary listened to Elizabeth, she knew that their quiet, ordinary life was over now. She drew a deep breath and squared her shoulders. *Yes,* she told God. *Do whatever You want in our lives.*

Immediately after His baptism, Jesus left home for over a month.

"Where is He?" their neighbors asked Mary and Joseph. "Where has He gone?"

"He went to be alone in the wilderness," Joseph told them quietly. But when he and Mary were alone, he asked her, "Will He be like John now, do you think? Living alone in the wilderness, dressing oddly, eating insects?"

Mary shook her head. "I do not know."

But after forty days, Jesus came home. He looked tired and thin, and Mary could see clearly that strong, resolute part of Him that she had only glimpsed before. And yet His love and gentleness still lit His face the same as always. She hurried to cook Him a good meal, a little shy of this thin Man whose eyes burned in His sun-browned face.

But then He laughed and hugged her, and He was her own Jesus again. "That smells wonderful," He said as she dropped pieces of lamb into the hot oil.

"You must be hungry." She looked at Him over her shoulder. "Weren't You lonely out there all those days?"

He shook His head. "I wasn't alone."

She wiped her hands and turned to face Him. "Who was with You?"

"The animals." He smiled. "And the angels."

After that Jesus was seldom home. He had a group of friends who traveled with Him, and Mary was glad He was not alone as He had been while He was in the wilderness, but she missed her Son. Her heart was heavy with sorrow and fear, for she was certain that nothing would ever be the same again.

The old days of quiet closeness with her son were over forever. He belonged to others now, and she would never be close to Him again. And she feared for Him, uneasy now that she could no longer feed Him and care for Him, making certain He was safe and well.

During the time that Jesus was away, Joseph became sick and died, breaking Mary's heart. Of course Jesus came home for His father's funeral, but He brought His disciples with Him, and Mary had no chance to be alone with Him. She felt sick with grief and resentment as she watched Him leave her home. "Why should I say yes to You, Lord," she muttered, "when You have taken both my husband and my son from me no matter what I say?" She bit her lip, ashamed of her anger at God, wishing she could talk to Joseph or Jesus about her feelings. But they were both gone, and she was alone.

The days were long and heavy for Mary. But she was looking forward to the wedding of Jacob and Rachel, Jesus' childhood friends, for she knew that Jesus was sure to be there. Maybe she would even have a chance to spend some time with her son.

At the wedding, Mary was glad to forget her sadness as she celebrated with Jacob and Rachel and their families and friends. Halfway through the party, though, she saw Jacob's father frown as he leaned close to his wife and said something in her ear.

"Oh no!" Jacob's mother looked around helplessly.

"What is it?" Mary asked her softly.

She hesitated, then whispered, "We've run out of wine." Her forehead puckered. "I knew we should have bought more, but. . ." She shrugged, tears in her eyes.

Mary touched her arm gently. She understood how expensive a wedding feast could be, especially for a family who had little extra money. Her heart ached for the bridegroom and his family, for the guests would not be happy when they discovered that the wine was gone.

Automatically, as she always had when her heart was troubled, she sought out Jesus. "They have no more wine," she told Him quietly.

He looked at her with understanding in His eyes, but His words were brusque. "How does that concern you and Me? My time has not yet come."

Mary looked at Him for a moment, surprised. She had not thought that He would necessarily solve the problem; she had merely wanted to tell Him what was wrong, for she had known that He would somehow make things better, just as He always did.

Over the years she had grown accustomed to sharing all her problems with Jesus, but since He had left home, she had begun again to deal with her troubles on her own. That was why her heart was so heavy lately, she realized. She had felt so alone, but she didn't have to, she saw. The time had come for others to share the great gift God had given her—but she could still tell her troubles to Jesus, just as she always had.

"I have missed You, Son," she told Him.

He smiled. "Look in your heart, Ema. I am with you always, forever."

Tears sprang to Mary's eyes, but she squared her shoulders and lifted her head high. As clearly as if a voice spoke to her out loud, she knew what she should do next. She turned to the servants who stood nearby. "Do whatever He tells you," she told them. She laughed to herself. "Say yes to whatever He says."

Jesus gave her a small smile. "It is My time, isn't it?" His eyes traveled around the courtyard, and then He pointed to the line of six stone water pots that stood along the edge of the wall. "Fill the jars with water," He told the servants.

The servants muttered to each other, their eyebrows raised. They looked from Jesus to His mother, and something they saw in their faces must have convinced them. Without another word, they filled the jars to the brim.

"What is He doing?" a friend whispered to her, but Mary only shook her head. She watched her Son, waiting to see what He would do next. She had learned long ago that when she brought a problem to Him, she needed to simply wait for Him to act in His own time and in His own way. If she came with a solution already in her mind, she was usually disappointed—but in the end, she always realized that He had known best all along.

Jesus leaned over the jars of water. He made no movement, spoke no word, but simply looked down into the clear water. He turned back to the servants. "Please," He said, "dip some out and take it to the master of ceremonies."

Mary watched as the master of ceremonies tasted from the cup. The man's eyes lit, and he motioned to the bridegroom to come to him. "Usually a host serves the best wine first," he said loudly. "Then, when everyone is full and doesn't care, he brings out the less expensive wines. But you have kept the best until now!" He clapped the groom on the back and laughed out loud, then took another deep drink of the wine.

After the wedding, to Mary's delight, Jesus spent a few days with His family. This time she did not mind that He brought His disciples with Him. They were good men, and she found herself laughing at Peter's jokes and enjoying John's quiet understanding. But she was grateful one night when Jesus joined her on the roof, and they sat together alone in the darkness, looking up at the stars as they had done so many times when Jesus was a child.

After a moment she broke the silence. "This is Your time now, isn't it, Son?"

"Yes." He tipped His head back against the stone wall and stretched out His long legs. "I must get busy now with My heavenly Father's business." He turned toward her, and she felt His eyes search her face in the darkness. "But I am sorry if it pains you, Ema."

She shook her head. "You are the Messiah, Son. I always knew that. Your earthly father would be proud of You, as I am."

She saw the flash of His white teeth. "People expect the Messiah to liberate Israel from Rome. Is that what you expect, Ema?"

For a long moment she gazed up at the bright stars, wondering what it was that she expected. She had feared the future for a long time, she realized, ever since Jesus was a baby, as though the future held some dark, horrible secret that would be too terrible for her to face. She remembered again the third astrologer's strange gift of myrrh, and she shuddered. And then she thought of Gabriel's bright face, and the calm, certain joy she had seen in his eyes. She sighed.

"I have learned, Son, that You and Your Father seldom do things the way I expect. I think my ways would be better—but in the end, Your ways are far better than anything I could ever imagine. So I might as well say yes from the very beginning— and then just wait and see what miracle You will do."

"Like you did at the wedding."

She smiled and nodded. "Yes." She looked at Him through the darkness. "Why did You do it? Why did You turn the water into wine? Such a little thing for You to bother with, such a small way for You to reveal Yourself."

Again she saw the gleam of His white teeth in the darkness. "Little things are important to My Father."

He reached for her hand. "The future will not be easy for you, Ema. But do not stop saying yes."

CHAPTER 11

"No!"

Three years later, Mary stood at the foot of a cross on Skull Hill, gazing up at her son. Around her people laughed and jeered and shouted insults. "No," she cried again, longing to silence them. She tipped her face up toward the strange purple sky. "You cannot let this happen, Lord. He is Your Son. How can You turn Your face and let Him die this way?" Her words dissolved into tears; she turned her head into her sister's shoulder.

The days that had led up to this afternoon had been like a nightmare. Joseph had been right to fear the government all those years ago when Jesus was just a baby, for in the end it was the government that had sentenced Jesus to death. Jewish religious leaders had done their part, though. They had formed a trap that had closed tighter and tighter around Jesus, until at last it shut tight on Him. But until the last moment, she had believed that He would somehow work a miracle and turn things around. She had not believed He would end up here, dying on a cross with two criminals.

Her sister held her close, but her arms were shaking. Beyond her, Mary caught a glimpse of the stricken faces of Mary Magdalene and Salome. And then she felt a gentle hand on her shoulder. She turned and looked into John's face.

"He wants to speak to you." His face was drawn, but his

brown eyes were steady and full of compassion. "Come."

Mary pulled away from her sister and moved closer to the cross. She could hardly bear to see the nails that pierced her son's skin; she longed to wipe the blood from His face and mend His wounds. But she could do nothing. *How can You do this, God? If I had the power, I would take Him home and heal Him; I would rescue Him and keep Him safe forever. I have no power to do that—but You do. How can You allow this to happen? He is Your Son, too. Don't You love Him, as I do? Aren't You a God of love? I don't understand.*

She swallowed back her tears and tipped her face up toward Jesus. "Son." Her voice quavered, but she hoped He would hear all her love in that one word.

"Ema." The familiar syllables brought fresh tears to her eyes. Through the watery blur, she saw that His face was tight with pain, but His eyes were filled with the same quiet love she had always seen there. She reached out to Him, longing to touch Him.

"Let John be your son now, Ema," He said. His gaze moved to John. "She will be your mother now."

John put his arm around Mary's shoulders. "Yes, Lord. Do not worry for Your mother. I will take care of her. And I will love her as my own mother."

Mary gazed up at her son, trying to understand why this horrible thing was happening. He had the power to get down from the cross all by Himself, she knew, for she had seen the miracles He could do. She thought of His friend Lazarus, whom He had raised from the dead. And then there had been the little girl, and Peter's mother. Each of these people He had saved from death's dark hold. And yet He was allowing Himself to be killed; He was saying yes to a criminal's death. "Why?" she whispered. "Why?"

But He did not hear her, or if He did, He gave her no answer. "I am thirsty," she heard Him say.

She longed to get Him a cup of cold water; she remembered all the nights when He was small, when she or Joseph had gotten up to bring their son a drink. Now, she could do nothing for Him. Dazed, she watched as someone soaked a sponge with sour wine, then stuck it on the end of a long branch and lifted it so Jesus could suck the moisture from it. He tasted it, then threw back His head.

"It is finished!" His head slumped forward. Her son was dead.

The rest of that long day was a blur for Mary. The crowd that had gathered slowly dispersed, but she and John and the other women stayed, watching that motionless body hanging from the cross. Soldiers came and broke the legs of the other two men who were being killed with Jesus, and Mary was oddly relieved when the soldiers left her son's quiet body alone. She flinched, though, when one of them thrust his sword into Jesus' side.

Finally, John led her gently away and brought her to his house. He gave her something to eat, but she only sat at the table, not eating, not thinking, staring dully at a small beetle that was crawling along the edge of the tabletop.

Suddenly, she jumped up.

"His body! What will happen to Him now? We must go get Him. Where will we bury Him?"

John shook his head and pushed her gently back into her chair. "Joseph of Arimathea has gotten permission from Pilate to take Jesus away. Joseph has a new tomb where he will bury Him. And Nicodemus has brought myrrh and aloe to embalm Him—and a long piece of linen to wrap Him in."

Mary's mouth twisted. "Myrrh," she said bitterly. "I hate myrrh."

John shrugged his shoulders helplessly. "I wish I knew how to comfort you."

Mary looked up at him and saw the tears that slid down his own cheeks. She shook her head. "No one can comfort us now. Jesus is dead." The words made her gasp with fresh pain.

"Yes." John's voice was heavy with sorrow. "But Jesus promised us that He would send us the Holy Spirit to comfort us. Remember what He said?"

Mary shook her head, barely listening to John's words, too overwhelmed with her pain.

John looked off into space, remembering. "This is what He said, Mary. Listen: 'If you love Me, obey My commandments. And I will ask the Father, and He will give you another Comforter, who will never leave you. He is the Holy Spirit, who leads into all truth. The world at large cannot receive Him, because it isn't looking for Him and doesn't recognize Him. But you do, because He lives with you now and later will be in you. No, I will not abandon you as orphans—I will come to you. In just a little while the world will not see Me again, but you will. For I will live again, and you will, too.' "

Mary shook her head. "How can He live again? I don't understand what He meant. We don't know how to work the miracles He did for Lazarus and Peter's mother."

John sighed. "No. We don't." He took her hand. "Come. I have a bed prepared for you. Try to get some rest."

Mary lay in bed staring into the darkness hour after hour. She felt as though someone had stabbed her through the heart, and she remembered the old man's prophecy so many years ago: A sword will pierce your very soul. Well, Simeon had been right about that. But why? Why had God sent His Son only to allow Him to be killed?

"No," she muttered. "I will not say yes to You this time, Lord. Whatever I say will make no difference. Jesus will still be dead. But I will not say yes to my son's death."

At last she fell into a fitful sleep, but her dreams were troubled and dark. Toward morning she woke up and lay staring at the window, a light gray square against the darker wall.

But it will make a difference.

She had fallen asleep again, she realized, but this time she felt a sense of peace steal into her heart. And the voice she heard speaking in her dream was Jesus'.

"What will make a difference?" she asked Him.

In the dream, He sat down cross-legged beside her sleeping mat and smiled down at her. *You know what I mean, Ema. It will make a difference whether you say yes or no to My death. It will make a difference in your own heart and in your own life. God can turn even the darkest, most horrible thing into something amazing and glorious, something far better than anything you could ever imagine. But first you have to say yes.*

"Not this time," she told Him. "I can't say yes to You being dead. I could never see anything good in Your death. Never."

Yes, Ema. You can.

"No. This is the worst thing that ever happened to me. It is the worst thing that ever happened in the entire world, ever. Worse than when our people suffered in slavery in Egypt, worse even than when our father and mother, Adam and Eve, first sinned in the Garden. You are the Son of God. And they killed You." Mary choked on the words.

Yes. And it is the worst thing that ever happened. But it is also the best thing. It is the reason that I came.

In her dream, Mary frowned. "How can that be?"

Don't you remember what I said? God loved the world so much that He sent Me, His only Son, so that everyone who believes in Me will never die, but will live forever.

He had said that, Mary remembered now. "But why did You have to die? Couldn't You have saved the world without dying?"

He shook his head. *No. I had to give everything.* He smiled and touched her face. *Don't be sad, Ema. I am leaving you with a gift of peace—peace of mind and heart. And the peace I give isn't like the peace the world gives. So don't be troubled or afraid. Remember what I told you: I am going away, but I will come back to you again. If you really love Me, you will be very happy for Me, because now I can go to the Father, Who is greater than I am.*

He took her hand in His. *Say yes, Ema,* He whispered, and then He was gone.

Mary opened her eyes. She didn't think she had dreamed a vision, as Joseph used to so long ago when the angel had spoken to him in his sleep. No, hers had been an ordinary dream—but she remembered now that during the days before His death, Jesus had really spoken the same words that He had in her dream. She just hadn't understood then.

The window was now a bright square of blue sky, and sunlight flickered across the earth floor beside her bed. Tears still leaked out of her eyes, but she drew in a deep breath and whispered, "Yes." And then she sat up and said it more loudly, "Yes! I am the Lord's servant, and I am willing to accept whatever He wants."

Mary was just as sad the next day, but despite her sadness, she continued to say yes to God in her heart. She and John talked quietly, remembering things Jesus had said. When she went to bed that night, she fell asleep at once and slept without any dreams.

In the morning she got up and began preparing food for the day. As she busied herself with ordinary household tasks, she sang psalms, despite her heavy heart. And then as she and John sat down to their morning meal, Mary Magdalene burst into the house. She stood panting, her face troubled and confused.

"What is it?" John asked in surprise.

When Mary Magdalene had caught her breath enough to speak, she gasped, "They have taken the Lord's body out of the tomb, and I don't know where they have put Him!"

About three months later, Mary knelt with a group of Jesus' believers, praying together as they did every day now. As they prayed, Mary thought back over all that had happened since that dark afternoon when Jesus had died.

Her son had risen from the dead! She could still barely grasp the miracle that had happened. They had lain Him in a grave, but death could not keep Jesus. When John had gone with Peter to see if what Mary Magdalene had said was true, they found an empty tomb. The linen cloths that had wrapped Jesus' body were neatly folded and lying on the stone shelf, and their hearts had been filled with a wild impossible joy. Jesus had conquered death forever.

After that, first Mary Magdalene had seen Jesus, and then He had come to His disciples. In the end, about five hundred people had seen Him, including His mother.

Mary remembered how wonderful it had been to be with her son again. Sometimes His death had seemed like a bad dream that she could forget all about. But she knew that His death was no dream. Because Jesus had loved the world enough to die, everyone who believed in Jesus would one day live with Him for eternity.

She had longed to keep Him with her, to go back to the old days when He was only her son, not the world's Messiah. But He had warned her that He could not stay with her. "Don't cling to Me," He had told her. "Soon I must ascend to the Father."

She hadn't understood what He meant—but by then she knew that Jesus might do anything at all. She couldn't predict His behavior. She certainly couldn't control Him. All she could do was nod her head. "Yes, Lord," she murmured, and His smile was her reward.

But many of the disciples still hoped that Jesus would free Israel from Rome after all. They kept asking Him, "Now will You restore our kingdom to us?"

Each time they asked the question, Jesus merely shook His head. "The Father will decide when your earthly freedom will come," He told them patiently. "He is the One who sets those dates, and they are not for you to know. But when the Holy Spirit has come upon you, you will receive power and will tell people about Me everywhere—in Jerusalem, throughout Judea, in Samaria, and to the ends of the earth."

Soon after that, one day when they were all talking with Jesus up on the Mount of Olives outside Jerusalem, He was suddenly taken up into the sky. As they watched, He disappeared into a cloud. Mary strained her eyes to catch one last glimpse of Him, her heart overwhelmed with joy and sorrow and wonder. And then some change in the light made her turn around.

Two white-robed men stood there among them, their skin glowing like gold. "Gabriel!" she cried.

He smiled at her, and then he turned to the apostles. "Men of Galilee," he said to them, "why are you standing here staring at the sky? Jesus has been taken away from you into heaven.

And someday, just as you saw Him go, He will return."

After that, all of Jesus' followers had begun meeting together every day in the upstairs room of the house where many of them were staying. Some of them thought they were waiting for Jesus' return, as the angel had promised, but Mary had a feeling that they were waiting for something else, something she could not imagine. After all, her Son never did things exactly the way she expected. He always took her by surprise.

Now, as they knelt together praying, she suddenly had a feeling that the thing for which they were waiting was about to happen. She raised her head, listening.

At first, all she heard was a tiny whisper, like a breath of wind blowing through the open window. John heard it, too, she saw; his eyes met hers, and she saw the same awe and delight there that filled her own heart. Soon the noise grew louder, until heaven roared with wind. The storm swept through the house.

Mary watched in wonder as flames of fire settled on each person in the room. She felt the burning heat on her own head and in her own heart.

This was the Holy Spirit, she realized, the Comforter whom Jesus had promised He would send. She could feel Him knocking on her heart's door, and she understood that by His power, God's great house would be built across the entire world, down through the ages. This was the kingdom her Son had come to build, not an earthly one as so many had hoped. As always, His plans were far greater than theirs.

And she would be a part of her son's amazing kingdom,

God's endless mansion of love. All she had to do was say that one familiar word. "Yes!" she cried and flung wide her heart's door. And the Holy Spirit came in and filled her with His power.

If you enjoyed

check out these other great
Backpack Books!

GIRLS' CLASSICS
Including *Pocahontas,*
Little Women,
Pollyanna, and *Heidi*

BIBLE HEROES
Including *Noah, Joseph,*
David, and *Daniel*

MODERN HEROES
Including *Corrie ten Boom,*
Eric Liddell, Billy Graham,
and *Luis Palau*

GOD'S AMBASSADORS
Including *Hudson Taylor,*
David Livingstone, Gladys
Aylward, and *Jim Elliot*

CHRISTIAN ADVENTURES
Including *Ben-Hur,*
The Pilgrim's Progress,
Robinson Crusoe, and
The Swiss Family Robinson

AMERICAN HEROES
Including
Roger Williams,
Abraham Lincoln,
Harriet Tubman
and *Clara Barton*

THE SON OF GOD
Including *Jesus,*
The Miracles of Jesus,
The Parables of Jesus,
and *The Twelve Disciples*

Great reading at a great price—only $3.97 each!

Available wherever books are sold.
Or order from
Barbour Publishing, Inc.
P.O. Box 719
Uhrichsville, Ohio 44683

If ordering by mail,
please add $2.00 to your order for shipping and handling.
Prices are subject to change without notice.